Tending the Fire

An Introspective Guide to Zen Awakening

TENDING THE FIRE

An Introspective Guide to Zen Awakening

DALE & BARBARA VERKUILEN

FIRETHROAT PRESS, LLC
MADISON, WISCONSIN

Published by Firethroat Press, LLC
2789 Marledge Street
Madison, WI 53711-5257
Web: www.firethroatpress.com
Email: info@firethroatpress.com

ISBN: 978-0-9830972-2-8

Library of Congress Cataloging Number: 2011946171

Publisher's Cataloging-In-Publication Data
(Prepared by The Donohue Group, Inc.)

Verkuilen, Dale.
Tending the fire : an introspective guide to Zen awakening / Dale & Barbara Verkuilen.
p. : ill. ; cm.
Includes bibliographical references.
ISBN: 978-0-9830972-2-8
1. Zen Buddhism. 2. Zen Buddhism--Philosophy. 3. Introspection. 4. Suffering--Religious aspects--Buddhism. I. Verkuilen, Barbara. II. Title.
BQ9288 .V47 2012
294.3/927 2011946171

Editor:
Joan Donovan, Ivory Bridge Editorial Services
ivorybridgecontact@yahoo.com

Book design and layout:
Kira Henschel, www.HenschelHAUSBooks.com

Cover design and graphics:
Aaron Gilmore, www.gilmoreart.com

Printed in the United States of America.

To the memory of David Grove
1950 – 2008

More and more in relation to the situation of our time,
I see the key to spiritual totality
is to be found in the psychophysical problem.
—Wolfgang Pauli

Contents

Note to the Reader i
Acknowledgments iii

Preface 1
Chapter 1: Tending the Fire 7
Chapter 2: Nonduality 19
Chapter 3: Nonduality – Resolution Sequence 39
Chapter 4: The Natural Koan 69
Chapter 5: Employing the Resolution Sequence 85
Chapter 6: *Shikantaza* 111

Appendix: Introduction to Metaphor Awareness 119
Metaphor Map for "Trepidation" 130
Case Study – 1991 to Present 149

Endnotes 163
Bibliography 169

About the Authors 173

Note to the Reader

This book contains five figures that correspond to Chapters 2, 3, 4, 6, and the Appendix. Larger versions of each are available as a free download at www.firethroatpress.com/downloads.

Acknowledgments

Many thanks:

To the Stray Dog Sangha—you know who you are—for the two-year study that helped refine the material presented in this book.

To Joan Donovan at Ivory Bridge Editorial Services [and Sr. Thelia] for thorough editing, and suggestions that improved the readability of the ideas we hope to convey in this work.

To Kira Henschel at HenschelHAUS Publishing for expertise in book design and layout.

To Aaron Gilmore at Gilmore Art for cover design and Metaphor Map illustrations.

To Dave Peters for the unglamorous task of advance reader/ proofreader.

—Dale and Barbara Verkuilen

PREFACE

There are many wonderful resources on Zen Buddhism. They range from the highly academic, to beautiful translations of the poetry of ancient Zen Masters, to books of Zen cartoons. Our bookshelves are filled with them. The subject seems well covered. Why write another one? What more could or should be added to the august body of knowledge already available on Zen? We asked ourselves these questions when undertaking the writing of this book. And yet, we were motivated to present the material contained here.

This work is unlike the others on our bookshelves in the fact that it addresses one aspect of Zen studies that does not seem to be covered by them. Its focus will be dedicated to understanding, working with, and resolving conditioned states. Buddhism acknowledges conditioned states as a major contributor to human suffering. The term for this suffering in Buddhism is *dukkha*, and it has three major components: ordinary suffering, impermanence, and conditioned states, on which more will be said later. It is the position of this work that conditioned states can and should be worked on directly as a central concern in the process of awakening.

With *Tending the Fire: An Introspective Guide to Zen Awakening,* we hope to offer an in-depth look at the process of awakening from a Western perspective, that can serve as a "how to" manual for the Zen practitioner. It is the outcome of forty years of exploring Zen practice and more than twenty years collaboratively studying the innovative psycholinguistic work of a "gentle genie" by the name of David Grove [1950-2008].

It is commonly known that the Dharma changes, and is changed, by its encounters with various cultures. The essential teaching is preserved though the forms may evolve so that it is more accessible to different peoples. A prime example of this is the stark variation between Indian Buddhism and the advent of Ch'an Buddhism developed during the highly creative T'ang dynasty, in China.

We are fortunate in the West that most schools of Buddhism are represented in an unprecedented fashion. More than likely, one can find a center or temple in the United States for any form of Buddhism now practiced in the world. There is much cross-fertilization between them as seekers endeavor to learn about the Buddha's teaching.

Buddhism has been studied scientifically, through the efforts of individuals like Richard Davidson and the Dalai Lama, to verify the benefits of meditation. Western psychotherapies have incorporated aspects of Buddhism, especially mindfulness practices, through the works of Jon Kabat-Zinn and others.

These efforts are examples of how the *Buddhadharma* has influenced the West. *Tending the Fire: An Introspective Guide to Zen Awakening*, illustrates the other side of the equation: how an essentially Western approach may impact the Dharma.

A major tenet of Buddhism is that our original nature is pure, and that we all are endowed with inherent enlightenment. Frankly, that is oftentimes difficult to observe in the world. But more than twenty years ago, as one of us [Barbara] was beginning her practice as a psychotherapist, she had the good fortune to attend the first of many trainings with David Grove. The study and use of his work verified the truth of Buddha's pronouncement on purity: as one worked symbolically with conditioned states, one witnessed the inherent become actualized.

David Grove was a creative teacher and therapist who employed innovative methods of psychotherapy. His earliest work was called *Metaphor Therapy*, a direct way of transforming conditioned states through their metaphorical equivalents. In this modality, metaphors are seen as the means by which negative learning is stored as a symptom in the body. By a precise and nonintrusive method of investigation, metaphors arise and provide form and clarity to one's psychic landscape. The process continues to gently "interrogate" the metaphor until the information embedded within is released, and the metaphor transforms. The metaphorical transformation correspondingly alters an individual's state of being, and one experiences a concomitant freedom from the afflictive emotions associated with a particular conditioned state.

The next evolution of his work was called the *Cosmology of Space*, where an individual learned how to map and change how his or her own conditioning was projected into the world. Before his death, Grove completed *Emergent Knowledge*, a self-directed method for accessing intuitive wisdom. With Emergent Knowledge, he succeeded in developing a method that was not necessarily facilitator-dependent. It is information-centered, and the information resides solely within the individual.

Grove's particular genius was evidenced in the way he closely observed all aspects of another person when communicating with that individual. Of course, he listened to what the person was saying, but he was more interested by the person's idiosyncratic gestures, sighs, and even vocal pauses, and the information these contained. His methodologies are all focused on how to elicit such nonverbal information. He understood that every mannerism of an individual was the manifestation of that individual's whole being, and that the information it contained could be used for healing and transformation. Oh, how very Zen! Grove proved to be a great "Zen" teacher without having the slightest interest in the subject.

To work with any of Grove's methods, an individual had only to pay close attention to her own experience through directed intention and nonjudgmental attention, as well as learn to trust the information that presented itself. These are the very same skills necessary for meditation, especially suited to *shikantaza* [just sitting] as practiced in Soto Zen.

Tending the Fire is a succinct distillation of our combined understanding of Grove's innovations and Zen training. Although the material presented is an adaptation, and takes his work in an entirely new direction, the authors must acknowledge that studying his groundbreaking modalities was of great significance in its development, primarily Chapter 3 on the Resolution Sequence. Our study of his work was also vital to our understanding of the origin, operation, and resolution of condition states.

We found Grove's work to be the perfect complement to our study and integration of Buddhism because it answered the needs of our Western psychology. Combining Zen practice with the introspective process outlined in *Tending the Fire* for resolving conditioned states, enhances a practitioner's understanding of the awakening process, one that rewards her with significant gains in freedom.

Chapter 1

TENDING THE FIRE

Years ago, our teacher Dainin Katagiri Roshi told the following story at a retreat. It was a rare occasion, in that he related a personal story about his early experience as a Zen priest. He said that although he had been raised a Buddhist, his family practiced Shin Buddhism, not Zen. But he had a strong motivation to become a Zen priest. Eventually he realized this desire.

Following his ordination he lived at a small temple with his teacher. He laughed as he confessed that within a few short months he became quite disillusioned about what it meant to be a Zen priest. He said he found it to be a really difficult life, and soon began to imagine going back to work at his family's restaurant. "But I had a problem," he said. "I didn't know how to tell my teacher I wanted to leave."

As time passed, he became more convinced that returning home was the right choice. Eventually, and with a great deal of anxiety, he got up the nerve to finally tell his teacher of his decision. His teacher listened attentively to the reasons he gave for wanting to leave. After Katagiri Roshi finished, his teacher said, "If that's what you need to do." Katagiri was surprised by how easily that had gone, and said if he had known that would be the response, he would have disclosed his decision a lot sooner.

Katagiri Roshi got up to leave, and just as he was about to exit the room, his teacher said, "*Dainin Sama*"... [The Japanese often add the suffix *San* after saying a person's name. It conveys courtesy and respect. When *Sama* is used, it reflects the highest regard for the person one is addressing.] His teacher said, "Dainin Sama, it will be the same wherever you go." Upon hearing his teacher's remark, he chose to stay.

This story is a modern-day example of the type of exchanges between masters and disciples, called *mondo*, that have been recorded throughout Zen's history. The title of this book is derived from another mondo, one from an ancient collection. Zen Master Dōgen relates it in the "Bendowa" fascicle of his *Shobogenzo—Treasury of the True Dharma Eye*.

A monk in Dōgen's assembly asked, "Once someone accepts that the *Buddhadharma* resides within all beings, what need is there for them to pursue the truth in Zazen?" [Nishijima and Cross, 2006] In response, Dōgen tells the monk about an old exchange between master and disciple that is summarized below.

At Master Hogen's monastery, there was a monk named Prior Soku. One day Master Hogen asked Soku how long he had been studying there. Soku answered that he had been at the monastery three years. Master Hogen then inquired, "In all that time, why have you not asked me a single question about the

Buddhadharma?" Soku responded, "I don't mean to mislead you. My questions were resolved while I was studying with Master Seiho, so I am content. Master Hogen asked, "By what means was this achieved?"

Soku answered, "I once asked Master Seiho: Just what is the student that is I?" Seiho said: "The children of fire come looking for fire."[1]

Master Hogen told Soku, "That's a nice saying but I fear that you have failed to understand it." Prior Soku then related to Master Hogen how he understood Master Seiho's comment. "Children of fire come looking for fire means that I don't need to search for myself when I already am myself."

Master Hogen then said, "Now I'm certain you misunderstand. If that is all that people gain of what the *Buddhadharma* has to offer, the truth would have been lost long ago." Soku was a bit humiliated by this critique of his understanding, and considered leaving the assembly. But a better inclination quickly arose. As a sincere student of Zen, Soku did not want to miss an opportunity to learn what Master Hogen might have to teach him.

So he asked Master Hogen, "Then tell me, Master, just what is the student that is I?" Master Hogen replied, "Children of fire come looking for fire." We are told that, upon hearing the answer this time, Prior Soku deeply understood the *Buddhadharma*. [Nishijima & Cross, 2006]

Katagiri Roshi's decision to stay after his teacher told him, "It will be the same wherever you go," and Soku's, "deeply understood the *Buddhadharma*," appear enigmatic when we hear or read about these stories. It leaves one to wonder, just what did they understand?

At the time Katagiri Roshi told his story, he didn't go into detail about why he decided to stay. But something in him was changed.

When Soku heard Master Hogen repeat, "Children of fire come looking for fire," and this time "deeply understood," something in him was changed.

It is this "change," and how to cultivate it, that is the focus of this book. To understand why the title *Tending the Fire* was chosen, it would be helpful to explore the mondo between Master Hogen and Prior Soku a bit further. Doing so will help introduce the content that follows.

Master Hogen rejected Prior Soku's initial understanding of Seiho's response, "Children of fire come looking for fire," because it missed the mark and did not go deep enough. Soku is challenged by this and asks Master Hogen his question, "Just what is the student that is I?" Master Hogen repeats the response Seiho originally gave him. Then we are told that Soku "deeply understood the *Buddhadharma*." Now we may ask, "By what means was this achieved?" What happened that made a difference between asking Master Seiho and Master Hogen, when the answer is the same?

Prior Soku's question, "Just what is the student that is I," is the essential concern of every Zen practitioner. It brings us back to Soku's first response to its meaning, which was, "I don't need to search for myself when I already am myself"—the one Master Hogen rejects. What is wrong with that answer? Are we not ourselves? Ah, therein lies the crux of Buddhism: "Just what is the student that is I?" Just what is the true nature of self? The liberating answer to his question, "Children of fire come looking for fire," directs our attention toward the deepest truths of human life. If we substitute reality for fire, we can begin to explore those deeper truths.

Children of fire [beings of reality] *come looking for fire* [come seeking the truth of reality]. This koan makes clear that it is necessary to gain more than an intellectualized understanding. There is a vital difference between inherent enlightenment [accepting as true that the *Buddhadharma* is within all beings] and realized enlightenment [experiencing that truth directly]. Achieving this difference is the imperative of Zen practice.

Tending the Fire: An Introspective Guide to Zen Awakening will focus on observing and overcoming the barrier between inherent and realized awakening. From here on, the term awakening will be used throughout this study, instead of enlightenment. The word enlightenment, unfortunately, invokes visions of a single, all-encompassing event, whereupon one imagines that no further effort is required. Awakening proposes a continuous process. Perhaps, awakening is the process by which enlightenment is achieved. There are many Buddhist texts that do entice us to believe in enlightenment with a capital "E." However, we have no experience with which to speak on that.

What we do know is that there is a fundamental misperception that is also innate to human experience. It is the default setting of our experience, naturally activated, and precisely what obstructs our inherent potential for awakening.

The fundamental misperception is that we experience ourselves as permanent entities separate from the world. Most human beings relate to the world as if it is made of "things" external to their experience that are enduring and can be manipulated, whereas Buddhism is a religion of relationships that teaches the interdependence of all phenomena. Interdependence, or dependent co-arising, is also called Emptiness. The term Emptiness expresses the impermanent nature of reality, and encompasses the understanding that no phenomenon has a permanent and independent existence.

This fundamental misperception of a permanent and independent existence is the Natural Koan of humanity. It lies at the core of our suffering, and is the essence that underlies the entire discourses of the Buddha and Zen masters. It is exactly articulated in the statement, "Children of fire coming looking for fire."

A *koan* is a question or problem that cannot be answered through our usual means of study or analysis. Thinking alone will not take us beyond the problem. Some other means to solve the dilemma must be found. The word natural, in *Natural Koan*, implies not only "usual" or "ordinary" but also the sense "of nature" in its meaning. Which is to say: not wrong, not inadequate, not sinful, but just a naturally arising event.

Although the Natural Koan of the fundamental misperception is common to everyone, each person manifests the problem it presents idiosyncratically, based on the unique circumstances of that individual's life. The Natural Koan wells up from the depth of our design. It has a distinct feeling-tone, one of alienation and discontentment: we find traces of it in all our experiences. It takes many guises. It is the basis of our dis-ease in the world. The fundamental misperception is a Universal quality in human life. How it plays out in each individual is the Personal aspect of one's experience. The terms Universal and Personal will be explored in greater depth in subsequent chapters, as they are relevant to the understanding of the fundamental misperception. [These terms and others to come will be capitalized, as they represent key concepts in the explanatory graphics.]

The Buddha is reported to have said, "I teach only one thing. I teach the nature and cessation of *dukkha*." [I teach the nature and cessation of suffering.] The Buddha also taught that *dukkha*, often translated as dissatisfaction, has three major causes.

The first cause of *dukkha* is the physical and mental pain that beings experience. It includes all the ways we suffer due to physical illness or incapacity, as well as mental suffering.

The second cause of *dukkha* is that the nature of reality is impermanence. Although that may give one hope in difficult times because one can count on the fact that things will change, it causes suffering when pleasant times turn troublesome.

The third cause of *dukkha* is conditioned states. Conditioned states are deeply rooted psychophysical formations predicated by negative experiences, and they are how we store negative learning. They arise as a way to mitigate difficult life events, but continue to influence our experience and behavior long after an event is over. Difficult life events are a subjective experience. They range from what an outside observer would consider mild, such as a child's experience of disappointing a parent, to what anyone would consider extreme, such as being in a war or natural disaster.

Posttraumatic Stress Disorder [PTSD] is an extreme example of a conditioned state. All conditioned states, including Posttraumatic Stress Disorder, are the natural result of living through mild to extreme negative events. There is no blame in it. Nor should there be shame. By the make-up of our nature, the conditioned state cannot help but arise.

A complex of afflictive emotions accompanies conditioned states, as well as habitual thought patterns and behaviors that manifest themselves in subsequent circumstances not in harmony with a new situation. They limit our freedom to respond to our life in ways we might prefer. A great deal of energy is expended in coping with conditioned states, but coping strategies do not alleviate the underlying root of the automatic response resulting from them.

When physical pain arises we can attend to it, but we do not have the option of never experiencing pain. Impermanence is the nature of reality. We cannot change the nature of reality, not that we don't try. Conditioned states are the one aspect of *dukkha* we can actively work with. *Tending the Fire* is dedicated to exploring conditioned states and their intimate relationship to awakening. It is the contention of this work that our effort in Zazen, combined with consciously working on conditioned states, is a vehicle for gaining liberation.

Zen Master Dōgen taught "practice is enlightenment." It is our understanding of his teaching that practice includes rigorous introspection and encompasses all our activity, not just Zazen [formal meditation].

Conditioned states are initiated by negative life events, although not all difficult circumstances create them. Once they are in play, however, they greatly influence how we respond to subsequent events similar to the original experience. A conditioned state is oftentimes experienced as, *well, that's just the way I am*, not that we wouldn't welcome being different. That is one way we can use to identify such a state. Conditioned states are the limiting tendencies we struggle against within ourselves. They are frustrating because no amount of intellectual understanding about why we are the way we are can lessen their impact. With a great deal of effort we manage ways to cope with them, some of the time. However, coping is not liberation. For liberation a transformative event must occur.

An apt, and potent, symbol in Buddhism is the lotus flower. Its seed is submerged in mud, but when the right conditions prevail the beautiful lotus blossom appears on the surface of the pond. Years ago scientists were studying the lotus flower because it has the unique ability to absorb dust and debris, yet allowing its blossom to always remain pure. The lotus flower can be understood as a symbol for transforming muddy conditions into wellsprings of beauty and purity. As such, it is the flower that best symbolizes awakening. The Buddha is sometimes referred to as the Lotus Flower of Humanity. When practitioners undertake the study of the impact of conditioned states and work to transform them through diligent practice, their efforts can be likened to the lotus plant's ability to perpetually purify the flower.

In the following chapters, you will be introduced to a symbolic representation of the awakening process. Each chapter will enhance the symbol as more information is introduced. The symbol is a precise way to convey large amounts of material in an organized and compact manner.

Chapter 2 will clarify Master Dōgen's unique perspective of radical Nonduality, the dynamic interplay of the Universal and Personal aspects of existence. Understanding Nonduality provides the framework for embracing wholeness, and wholeness is the medicinal necessary to impact the fundamental misperception. The Personal encompasses the relative aspects of our experience, which do not diminish. Instead, our ordinary experience is cradled in a vaster understanding when ameliorated through the perspective of the Universal.

Chapter 3 expands the information on Nonduality with the introduction of the Resolution Sequence. The Resolution Sequence is an introspective process for working with and resolving conditioned states. With its use, our efforts are engaged in the transformative process from the beginning, and are directly in line with Dōgen's pronouncement that "practice is enlightenment."

The Resolution Sequence consists of two equal parts, an investigative inquiry into one's problem[s], and integrating the liberating experience upon its solution. It can be viewed as a means for extending the benefit of meditation, as it aids with the organization of information, so that practitioners can assess their relationship to a problem by using its systematic model. What is essential throughout the process is a new orientation toward our limitations. With respect and curiosity toward the conditions of our life, we can relinquish our resistance to engaging with any issue.

The Resolution Sequence also offers the ability to enhance Zazen practice by engaging with the problem through the conscious use of thought. Once an individual has a stable meditation practice, the Resolution Sequence can be employed as a method for working directly with one's Natural Koan.

The multitude of koans used in Zen practice is the record of the existential dilemmas of our Zen ancestors. They are the record of the naturally arising inquiry of the individual practitioners as they encountered the conditions of their lives in relation to Buddha's teaching and Zen practice. Use of the Resolution Sequence to engage one's own existential question harkens back to the pure origins of Zen. One practices what Master Dōgen called "the koan realized in life."

Chapter 4 will discuss in more detail the meaning of Natural Koan as it is used within the context of this study. Earlier we stated that the fundamental misperception of separation is the Natural Koan of humanity. Chapter 4 will focus on how practitioners can use the Resolution Sequence to identify and work with conditioned states, the functioning of the fundamental misperception in their own lives.

Chapter 5 will provide narratives of three individuals who have successfully employed the Resolution Sequence, expanding the scope of circumstances by which it may be helpful. By these means, the process hopefully becomes less abstract and therefore more meaningful.

Chapter 6 will discuss *Shikantaza* as a practice after the integration of the understanding of the Resolution Sequence, and how it complements a practitioner's efforts in achieving freedom.

The Appendix includes three items: an introduction to the Metaphor Awareness process, an illustrated map of a Metaphor

Awareness session, and a twenty year Case Study exemplifying the results of creatively working with conditioned states in conjunction with traditional Zen practice.

The Natural Koan is our call to action; *Tending the Fire* is offered as a response to that call. It is a means by which we may tend to our life with the same diligence as would be needed to respond to an actual fire, say, one burning on a dry prairie of tall grasses heading toward our abode. Katagiri Roshi used to say, "Our life is an emergency situation."

Chapter 2
NONDUALITY

The goal of Zen practice is to see the world as it is and attain freedom. The practitioner accomplishes the goal when the fundamental misperception of viewing the world as separate and distinct from oneself is replaced with a thoroughgoing unitive vision of Nonduality.

Nonduality relieves the emotional distress of separation by seeing things, including oneself, as impermanent and transitory, with all existence arising from conditions that are related to all phenomena. Everything has dependent existence; everything depends on the support of the entire universe for its existence. Acquiring the understanding that an enduring self-nature is nonexistent unravels the false assumption that beings are "things." "Things" are judged correctly as provisional and ephemeral, without a self-nature apart from their contingent and complex network of support. Perceiving the world as an intricate net of "relationships" is central to understanding Nonduality. This net of relationships is a vast overarching matrix of changing conditions within which an individual's life is derived.

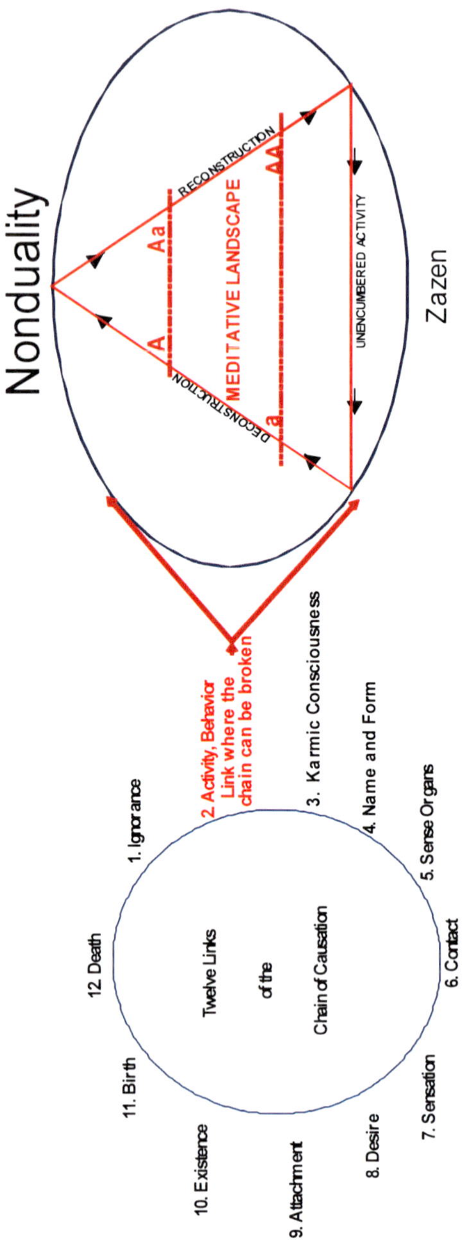
Nonduality
RECONSTRUCTION
DECONSTRUCTION
A
Aa
a
AA
MEDITATIVE LANDSCAPE
UNENCUMBERED ACTIVITY
Zazen
2. Activity, Behavior
Link where the
chain can be broken
1. Ignorance
3. Karmic Consciousness
4. Name and Form
5. Sense Organs
6. Contact
7. Sensation
8. Desire
9. Attachment
10. Existence
11. Birth
12. Death
Twelve Links
of the
Chain of Causation

FIGURE 1

With "things" now seen as not the final answer, and with "relationships" observed as the heart of awakening, new means of adapting to this truth must be developed. Dealing with relationships requires dealing with dynamic change. In addition, every individual has roots in both the Personal and Universal aspects of being. In other words, when addressing change and relationship, the entire makeup of an individual must be considered.

The symbol, Figure 1 titled "Nonduality," is an attempt to incorporate visually the process of dynamic change, the wholeness of being, and the wisdom of Nonduality. The purpose of the symbol is to provide support for the development of an individual undertaking Zen practice, and to act as a lifelong guide as one treads the path of awakening. The Nonduality Symbol is like most other symbols; it encapsulates a broad understanding of many concepts and processes into a shorthand yet meaningful visual form. It is an invitation to the practitioner to invest energy in exploring and attaining a wide and deep mastery of Buddhist thought and experience.

Symbols have the ability to concisely arrange and convey large amounts of knowledge. Symbolic depictions have the ability to open new vistas. A significant example of how the use of symbols brought enormous change occurred in the field of mathematics. The use of symbolic expression organized and ultimately replaced rhetorical terms. This creative insight and action subsequently opened the field to an unexcelled period of ingenuity.

Prior to the sixteenth century, algebra was expressed in a combination of words and numbers with just a few pioneering symbols. With problems addressed in this essentially rhetorical fashion, calculations were haphazard and not well defined. The sought-for unknown factor was either expressed with a complex series of drawings, or it required a level of abstraction unique to each individual problem. However, during the fifteenth, sixteenth, and seventeenth centuries, mathematical expression began to evolve from words to letters, moving the statement of problems deeper into the symbolic realm.

Alex Bellos, in his book on the history of mathematics, *Here's Looking at Euclid*,[2] gives this example of how a typical problem would be stated before the symbolic change was implemented:

4 in A quad – 5 in plano +3 aequator 0.

Descartes, the seminal French philosopher and mathematician, saw how the use of words inhibited quick and accurate solutions. He devised a system that replaced the rhetorical with single letters that represented the unknown, as well as other values. His simplification transformed the awkward French word statement of the above problem to this symbolic representation:

$$4x^2 - 5x + 3 = 0$$

The solution to the problem almost magically appears after the restatement. Embedding the assumption that "x" stands for the unknown unleashes the innate vigor of the symbol. Thought is freed from the limitations of language and explanation, allowing greater access to our intrinsic visionary mentality. Symbolic thought encompasses many concepts that appear at odds, revealing underlying relationships. The symbolic structure reveals the areas where they meet and relate. Mathematics began to develop with great speed after the refinement of algebraic expression using letters and other symbols. Many new mathematical systems and schemes of calculations have been produced since then, each of which has demonstrated the creativity sparked by Descartes and his colleagues. Innovative thinking, powered by symbols, continues to energize groundbreaking mathematical research and breakthrough insights to this day.

The Nonduality Symbol was conceived as an aid to organize one's life for awakening, moving it, like mathematics, from explanations centered upon concepts and freestanding insights into the realm of symbols. As will be shown, this symbol and subsequent variants of it offer a simplified path of determining what is helpful to an individual's awakening process. It is not intended to teach the Dharma directly. Rather, the symbol assembles the major features of the process in a graphical representation. Much like a mathematical graph that communicates data, the rate of change, amplitude, and direction of movement, the Nonduality Symbol illustrates gathered information, its importance, and what progress an individual has made. Without an organizational structure, the myriad bits of information from readings, lectures, reflections, conversations, meditative insights, and daily life may often confuse rather than shape a coherent understanding. Employment of the Nonduality Symbol helps to minimize uncertainty on how these categories operate together.

A Zen teacher once described Zazen as sitting at the foot of a mountain and then suddenly waking up at the summit. This is an accurate description of "sudden enlightenment." One moment the mind is engaged in its usual modes of consciousness, and then abruptly an unanticipated psychophysical shift occurs, bringing with it an entirely new sense of self and worldview. If one has access to competent instruction, this manner of practice can be constantly energized. However, without the recurrent creative input of a watchful teacher or a robust continuity of awareness, inspired resolution can be thwarted. Practice may lapse into quietism, or merely satisfaction with pleasant sensations and feelings that arise in Zazen.

Learning and employing the Nonduality Symbol can help keep the practitioner on track, even when a close relationship with a teacher is not at hand. The relationships contained within the symbol have the ability to paint a picture that is easily remembered and applicable to many varied internal and external life conditions. The symbol presents an opportunity to grasp the field of study as a whole, acting as a roadmap pointing the way, as well as providing a persistent stimulus against falling into naïve mental states. Resourceful introspection is an active contribution to the process of awakening. Zazen remains a vital inclusive activity, one that makes use of every human capability through its constant inquiry into the nature of self.

The Meaning of the Symbol's Elements

Figure 1, the Nonduality Symbol [shown on page 20] presents a new approach to understanding the practice of Zen awakening. Later chapters will expand on this foundation. Included below are descriptions of the individual parts of the symbol, along with an explanation of how each assists in creating a strong base for practice. Figure 1 contains the elements referred to in this section. The following will clarify the fundamental meaning of each section of the symbol.

The Twelve Links of the Chain of Causation

The Twelve Links of the Chain of Causation[3] provide a concise view of the cyclical nature of the causes and conditions that perpetrate the cycle of *dukkha*. Buddha taught that *dukkha* has no end, unless this cycle is understood and creative actions are taken to sever the Chain. Seeing ourselves and others as separate and independent beings is the misperception that supports the Chain of Causation. Without conscious intervention, the Chain arises and operates in our lives automatically. It begins with Ignorance and proceeds through Birth and Death, repeating itself again and again.

There are several causes that perpetuate Ignorance: failure to understand cause and effect, denial of the impermanent nature of the world and its interdependent origination, and the absence of an enduring self-nature. The diagram of the Twelve Links on Figure 1 indicates that Ignorance conditions activities and behaviors, which in turn bring about karmic consciousness. This in turn conditions a series of occurrences that ultimately results in entrapment in the cycle of Birth and Death.

Zazen uncovers the deep truth regarding the operation of the first two links. Of the three kinds of *dukkha* [physical pain, impermanence as the nature of reality, and conditioned states], this study centers on the cessation for the third one, conditioned states, and the afflictive emotions that arise from them. Mental afflictions arise when a stimulus activates a conditioned state. When some event [inner or outer] triggers a conditioned state and its associated emotions, an act of creative will is possible. If one does not recognize, or does not know how to interdict the negative outcomes of the conditioned state, the cycle of the Twelve Links of the Chain of Causation will proceed without any impediment to its unfavorable conclusion. However, the practice of Zazen offers conscious engagement with conditioned states at the 2nd Link, where the practitioner gains the possibility of breaking the cycle.[4]

The Expansion Lines

The expansion lines from the 2nd Link of the Chain of Causation show that the Nonduality Symbol is an enlargement of the activity possible at the 2nd Link. The symbol is a magnifying lens that exhibits in detail how to sever the Chain at that link. The information embedded in Ignorance manifests as a dizzying array of mental and emotional states that arise with speed and power. Amplification offers a chance to understand what is happening without being swept away. The more one becomes conscious of the attributes associated with a triggered conditioned state, the more one gains the ability to cut off the habitual response to it, thereby severing the Chain of Causation.

The Encompassing Ellipse

The ellipse encloses the entire symbol and all of its elements. It symbolizes Master Dōgen's inclusive teachings of Nonduality. All activities within the bounds of the ellipse are constituents of the nondual mind. Dōgen refuted the misunderstanding that our inherent nature and its tendency toward dualism should be ignored or repressed. Zazen is not a practice of minimizing or suppressing dualistic thought, even though this orientation is widely assumed to be the heart of practice. Rather, Dōgen acknowledged the development and refinement of all human abilities as essential in his teaching of what constitutes authentic practice. Nothing is left out of the practice of wholeness. Dōgen scholar Hee-Jin Kim refers to the activity of the dualistic elements within the sphere of Nonduality as "foci." He does so to emphasize that the dualistic elements are envisioned as acting as innate complements, not as oppositional elements that need to be blended into harmony through practice. Dōgen's wholeness is expressed in the nonfragmenting practice/realization of Zazen.[5]

Below are terms that may help in understanding Kim's use of the relationship of "foci" as the Personal and Universal expressions of the self. None of these terms taken individually completely describes the depth and complexity of dualistic relationships because their associations are complex and require significant effort to clarify. However, studying the pairings and their relationship creates an enhanced picture that aids in defining dualistic pairs as complementary.

Drawing an ellipse is another aid in understanding the way that the foci interact. A circle can be drawn from one point with a compass. An ellipse, however, requires two focal points to produce its shape. The distance between the foci determines the size and shape of an ellipse. Similarly, the ellipse depicted on the Nonduality Symbol demonstrates the relationship between the dualistic foci of the Personal and Universal aspects that makeup an individual

Dualistic Foci		Nonduality
Personal	Universal	Complementary Activity
Practice	Realization	*Shikantaza*, Zazen Only
Deconstruction	Reconstruction	Unencumbered Activity
Delusion	Enlightenment	Wholeness
Individual, Relative, Ordinary	Collective, Absolute, Ultimate	Unity
Psychological	Spiritual	Oneness
Form, Feelings, Perceptions, Impulses, Consciousness	Emptiness	Emptiness of Emptiness
Body, Subject	Mind, Object	Simultaneous Arising
Thinking	Not-thinking	Nonthinking
Being (Space)	Time	Continuum
Inquiry	Response	Radiant Knowledge

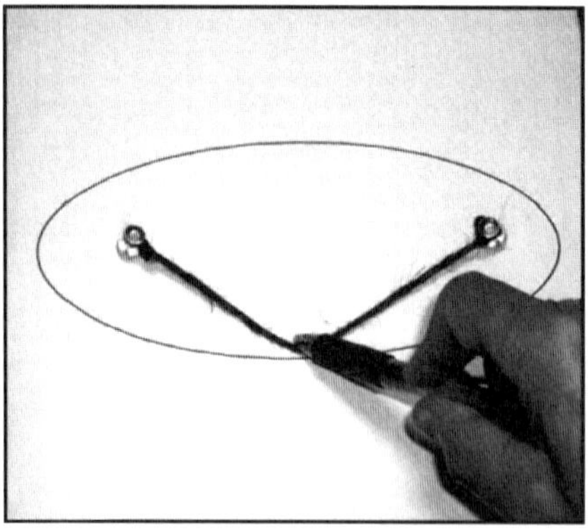

being. The Personal focus consists of the distinct and unique components of an individual. They are products of culture, education, nurture, volitional acts, and the immediate environment. The Universal focus is made up of collective and ultimate characteristics. This focus is defined as the shared action of the universe conditioning an individual's life, arising from the actions of all antecedent beings from deepest antiquity. The Personal and

Universal aspects of the self, taken together, give rise to the wholeness of an individual with the same dynamic complementary relation that the points of the ellipse achieve in generating its geometric completeness.

The ellipse pictured on the Nonduality Symbol represents the cumulative action of all the inherent dualities. The ellipse encloses all of the elements of the symbol, thereby illustrating two important points:

The two foci of the ellipse represent the two sides of dualistic thinking. They are complementary components acting in harmony to create the inclusive wholeness of Nonduality, even though they are normally sensed as opposites.

The mind of Nonduality does not transcend dualistic thinking. Rather Nonduality is the complementary sum of duality, and with knowledge and training, reshapes and refines dualistic thinking.

Meditative Landscape

The Meditative Landscape is the mind of the practitioner engaged in Zazen. Zazen means to collect the contents of the mind. The activity of Zazen dissolves unsubstantiated beliefs and offers the possibility of recognizing the psychophysical formations of conditioned states. Zazen has two aspects: tranquility and insight, and they operate both on and off the meditation cushion. They are the natural outcome of perseverant effort in Zazen, an experience wherein the quality of nonjudgmental acceptance naturally manifests. The major impetus for change results from a firm and long-standing application of effort in mastering the practice of Zazen.

The placement of the broken lines denoting the Meditative Landscape indicates transition points associated with an Awakening. Passing through a line indicates a growth of awareness that results in a revision of perspective, a transformation of being, or a radical change of behavior.

The Triangle and its Side Labels

The triangle symbolizes the path on which the awakening process advances. It indicates a self-contained course of development where the practitioner gathers preliminary experience and awakenings occur: an ongoing network where practice proceeds endlessly with ever-deepening opportunities.

The three sides of the triangle are the three divisions of the awakening process: Deconstruction, Reconstruction, and Unencumbered Activity.

Deconstruction differentiates the set of assumptions and habitual thinking patterns that comprise our conditioning. The process of Deconstruction is initiated by observing the operation of conditioned states that occurs within the sphere of Zazen, the Meditative Landscape. It begins when an individual recognizes that a problem exists within his/her life, and that conscious activity can resolve the problem. One then commits oneself to Zen practice. The ultimate outcome of Deconstruction is freedom from conditioned states. The apex of the triangle indicates a nondual mentality embodying freedom in an emerging form, a nascent liberation attained in sudden awakening that requires gradual cultivation to achieve its full potential.

Reconstruction is the integration of the information realized in Deconstruction. The process of Deconstruction moves from conditioning to freedom; Reconstruction is learning to live that freedom. In Reconstruction, the personality of the individual is imbued with freedom, reorienting one's skills and abilities and liberating the person from previous inhibitions, as well as opening up new avenues for individual and social creativity.

Unencumbered Activity results from successful completion of Reconstruction. Liberation from the effects of conditioned states is achieved after the conscious work of Deconstruction and Reconstruction. The ever-present beneficent enlightened mind replaces narcissistic thoughts and self-seeking behavior. The bottom line of the triangle indicates a nondual mentality embodying freedom in a mature form.

The Arrowheads

The path-pointer arrowheads indicate the direction of ceaseless dynamic movement, from the first conscious act of Deconstruction, through the integration of Reconstruction, to the freedom of Unencumbered Activity, and then on to subsequent efforts of resolution. They indicate that the practice/realization of inclusive Nonduality is a beginningless and endless continuous penetration of the truth of Zen teaching.

Awakenings

The four Awakenings are the critical moments where the great changes of one's life occur.

They are profound life-altering events that are the reward of conscious effort to manifest one's inherent enlightenment. As a young man, Dōgen questioned why practice was necessary if one is already Buddha. This question infused his life with energy that eventually led him to its resolution. He summarized his insight, echoing previous teachers in this line from the *Fukanzazengi*: "Think of not-thinking. How do you think of not-thinking? Nonthinking." Thinking and not-thinking are foci that when engaged in the practice of Zazen actualize nonthinking. Nonthinking and Nonduality express the same unified experience and can be understood as synonyms.

There are two categories of awakenings: perspective and transformative. Perspective awakenings ["a" "Aa"] modify the orientation of mind, enlarging the conscious view of the self and its constituents. Transformative awakenings ["A" "AA"] resolve conditioned states and reshape being and behavior.

Awakening "a"

Awakening "a" is a perspective that witnesses a conditioned state or a problem as it arises and unfolds. One gains the ability to observe the difference between being unconsciously trapped by a conditioned state and being consciously aware of how it manifests. This awareness is the beginning of what constitutes Dōgen's "not-thinking," that is to say, recognizing the conditioned thoughts as they come up, and beginning to see how to avoid the trap of making a habitual response. Not-thinking is the dawning of a new way of seeing, discovered and cultivated in Zazen. Dedication to the study of the Way becomes central to life's activities. Becoming aware of conditioned states makes articulation of one's idiosyncratic Natural Koan possible.

The mind of not-thinking advances awareness of the reality and interplay of ordinary dualistic pairs such as pleasure/pain, ambiguity/clarity, fondness/ill-will, and confidence/insecurity, as well as dualities requiring deeper insight such as delusion/ enlightenment, birth/death, or Buddhas/ordinary beings. They are seen to be what they are. Before Awakening "a," the self was considered an enduring "thing," with each transient thought and feeling considered to be the complete answer to the question, "Who am I?" or "What is the student that is I?" With continuing practice, the Universal viewpoint that opens in Awakening "a" expands and intensifies, disclosing the non-abiding impermanence of each element of the self. Awakening "a" matures from passive observation into an active embrace of the free-flowing mentality that the self is now seen to be.

Awakening "A"

Awakening "A" is the life-defining resolution of some aspect of the Natural Koan, the koan realized in life. A conditioned state at the bottom of the Natural Koan resolves itself suddenly, resulting in freedom from the afflictive emotional confinement associated with it. The conditioning and ingrained assumptions associated with it, previously taken as the authentic self, are overturned and no longer viewed definitively. An entirely new reference replaces the false notions of reified "things."

A breakthrough produces a transformation where the barriers to Nonduality drop away. The Universal, at this time, is now the dominant view, setting the stage where the impermanence of all beings [including oneself] and their fleeting existence becomes empowering rather than threatening. The change means a new understanding of the Buddhist principle of no permanent self. Furthermore, the paradox of the relationship between the many [Personal] and the one [Universal] is clarified in the sphere of Nonduality. In the complementary nondual activity of the Universal and Personal duality, the Universal and Personal retain their identities. They are seen at once to mutually interpenetrate and yet remain distinct. The pointed apex of the triangle symbolizes the leaping clear of ambiguity into Nonduality.

Awakening "Aa"

Awakening "Aa" is the ability to observe and begin the integration of the changes brought about by the psychophysical shift engendered by Awakening "A." The central issue in Reconstruction is to fully embody the change of being. It is accomplished by mastering the freedom of mind and body envisioned by Awakening "A." Awakening "Aa," like Awakening "a" is also a change of perspective. The focus is on the freedom from the afflictive emotions associated with a conditioned state, and on the ability to think and feel in entirely new ways. The individual engaged in this process perceives any lingering habit energies related to the resolved conditioned state as "uprooted." The process of Awakening "Aa" incorporates the insight gained in Awakening "A" into daily life.

Awakening "AA"

Awakening "AA" occurs when the changes realized from the Awakening "A" are completely integrated. The breakthrough produces a transformative change of behavior. The change of behavior accomplished in "AA" removes any vestige of negative habit energy, making responses to life natural and in accord with the needs of oneself and others. Peace and equanimity are found within ordinary events. Awakening "A" resolves the fundamental misperception of a separate and alienated existence. Completing Reconstruction is Awakening "AA," a total engagement with events and beings. Its truth is not found in transcending the problems of life. Rather, the path to freedom lies deep within all life, not in an escape from it. Cognizance of the mutual *Buddha-nature* verifies this point.

Zazen

Zazen is the central activity of Soto Zen Buddhist practice. It is not a method of self-improvement, or a way of attaining a healthy lifestyle while ignoring the needs of the world. Zazen surpasses mental, physical, and psychological well-being. These elements are, of course, important, but their cultivation should not be confused with the nondualistic practice of Zazen. The teaching of Zen points to the mind of Nonduality where confusion is dispelled, tranquility is born, and wisdom arises. According to Dōgen, the practice of Zazen is in itself realization. Awakening manifests directly within the immediacy of the moment, not as the ultimate reward for practice. Realization resides within the process of moment-by-moment awakening.

Working with the Nonduality Symbol exemplifies the three basic elements of awakening in Zazen contained in the geometric patterns.

First, with the meditative landscape at its center, the symbol communicates that emphasis on practice is essential. Zazen is the existential inquiry in action, from which experiential knowledge and wisdom are derived. Reflections, thought, and taking on other's opinions on the matter do not necessarily yield anything that is ultimately worthwhile in answering one's existential dilemma. However, in Zazen the unity of inquiry and immediate insight provides a resourceful way of approaching existential questioning. Engagement in Zazen sets the stage for the revolution of mind that cures the fundamental misperception of separateness.

Second, the triangle and arrowheads portray the dynamic movement of impermanence. The practice/realization of Zazen helps one shed the notion of a fixed self. Ongoing awareness of an endless stream of life cycles replaces the notion of the substantial and enduring self. Each fast-moving cycle contains both a unique problem based on the conditioning of the moment and the means to resolve it, and ultimately achieve liberation. Understanding and accepting the reality of the metabolism of this process transforms impermanence from a confining trap to an opportunity for ever-burgeoning freedom.

Third, the ellipse symbolizes the nondual complementary sum of the constant and vital interplay between the Personal and Universal aspects of life. The intimate interplay of the dualistic pairs is in itself Nonduality, the unfolding of the wholeness of being. The relationship of the body and mind in Zazen is an accessible example of the complementary interplay of a dualistic pair. When sitting, an erect posture results in an aware mind, which in turn promotes an even straighter posture and so forth, in an endless positive feedback loop. The practitioner recognizes Nonduality to be the complementary activity of the body-mind, embracing all of the complexities and ambiguities of dualistic relationships.

Chapter 3
NONDUALITY – RESOLUTION SEQUENCE

In Figure 2, shown on the following page, an introspective guide called the Resolution Sequence is added to the Nonduality Symbol. The sequence describes in detail the process of awakening from the first glimmer of awareness to its ultimate culmination. It is a skillful means that acts in accord with the practice of Zazen. Learning and applying its principles gives Zen practitioners the ability to understand where they are on the path.

The Resolution Sequence is made up of twelve stages that elaborate the processes of Deconstruction and Reconstruction. Following them to completion results in the freedom of Unencumbered Activity and opens the pathway to subsequent opportunity for resolving other life issues. Deconstruction identifies and resolves conditioned states; Reconstruction focuses on integrating the freedom found in the resolution of them.

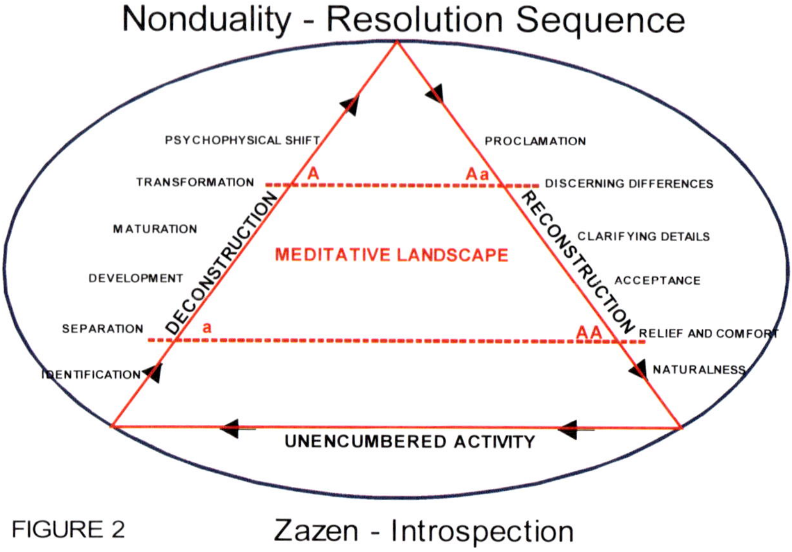

FIGURE 2

The Resolution Sequence is an expedient to self-discovery, reduces confusion, and also discloses a measure of progress. Without an outer teacher, the Resolution Sequence acts as an inner guide to minimize missteps and encourages diligence. Studied in combination with traditional Zen training methods, it promotes a deeper and more conscious understanding of the process of Zen awakening.

Some Western psychological systems have adapted Buddhist meditation techniques with positive results. Here, however, a Western introspective means has been shaped to aid recognition and appreciation of how the practice of Zazen operates to break the Chain of Causation. The Nonduality Symbol offers an expanded view of what breaking the 2nd Link means; the Nonduality-Resolution Sequence Symbol combines Zazen and introspection, thereby increasing the scope of Chapter 2.

The study of Nonduality is not directly concerned with intellectual understanding, self-improvement, or psychotherapeutic goals. It has only one aim: awakening, and the wisdom and compassion that issue from this life-changing process. Because the Resolution Sequence is an amplification of Nonduality, it maintains the same aspiration. We call this combination Zazen – Introspection, where Zazen is the practice of Nonduality, and Introspection is a detailed experiential study of the self with the aid of the Resolution Sequence.

It is essential to understand the nature of Zazen – Introspection and the relationship between them. Zazen, also known as *shikantaza* [just sitting], is nonjudgmental theme-less meditation that is in itself an inquiry into the true nature of self. Achieving the ability to "just sit" is an arduous task requiring years of study and practice. Practitioners encounter many obstacles that must be resolved. It is folly to think that one can engage in serious inquiry into the nature of self without understanding what these obstacles are, and how they manifest within one's life. Without a firm foundation of knowledge of Buddha's teaching combined with introspection, a practitioner can easily go astray. An intellectual study of the sutras and a conceptual approach to understanding the extensive Zen literature takes one to the gates of practice; Zazen – Introspection opens them.

The conventional understanding of introspection is contemplation, self-analysis, and examination of one's inner life.

However, it takes on an expanded meaning in Zen practice. Zazen – Introspection is analogous to koan introspection. In koan introspection, the practitioner studies a teacher-assigned koan within the meditation practice. The study consists of penetrating the inner meaning of the koan, thus gaining experiential insight. Such insight lights up the path past discursive thought and emotional dead ends, pointing directly to the awakened mind of Buddha. Zazen – Introspection offers the same intuitive acuity without the assigned koan.

The Natural Koan and its innumerable expressions replace the assigned koan. An individual's spiritual life revolves around a chief feature that recurs over and over in many different forms. The Natural Koan arises quite spontaneously in daily life. Instead of engagement with the piercing arrow of an assigned koan, the issue of one's commonly occurring concerns become the focus of the introspective drive. Zazen and introspection act as complementary dualistic foci, providing a core understanding of the problems as they arise, along with the creative direction and unifying information that is essential to resolve them.

Resolution Sequence

What follows below are definitions of the twelve stages of the Resolution Sequence as depicted in Figure 2. The sequence is divided into the sections of Deconstruction and Reconstruction.

Deconstruction – Moving from Conditioning to Freedom

The process of Deconstruction consciously engages with conditioned states that are rooted in negative learning stored as psychophysical formations. This effort, if taken through to completion, ultimately resolves these formations, freeing one from the suffering that arises from them. The process of Deconstruction moves from conditioning toward freedom. It brings about greater awareness of the complementary interplay between the Personal and Universal foci of wholeness, and offers a means to eliminate the barriers caused by conditioned states that impede the full freedom of that interplay.

The Six Stages of Deconstruction

1. Identification

The term Identification refers to the process of emerging from a mental landscape where conditioned states unconsciously dominate without interdiction. An individual becomes aware of the actions of conditioned states and the barriers to freedom they cause. A practitioner may experience various kinds of mental and/or physical pain, the sources of which are not clearly understood. The problem manifests as afflictive emotions, and their roots reside within the conditioned states. After becoming aware of these detrimental influences, one articulates a description of the problem, along with an intention to resolve it. This is the beginning of a Zen life.

Identification is characterized by the absence of questioning. Without reflection and inquiry, our unfolding life just happens within a single perspective, defined by whatever momentary perception is occurring. Life is on autopilot with little incentive or skill to regard one's experience in any other way. Some analysis is of course possible and necessary for living. One makes evaluations and judgments all the time in the conventional sense. However, when a nonreflective individual receives the suggestion that objects and events might be other than how they appear, or receives a proposal to formulate an inquiry such as, "How else could this circumstance be viewed?" he often vigorously rejects the possibility with statements such as, "That's just the way things are," or, "That's just the way I am." Other responses include denial that there is a problem, taking events and relationships for granted, defensiveness, and blaming others.

* * *

The next three stages of Separation, Development, and Maturation are experienced within the Meditative Landscape. Moving from Identification into Separation is the beginning of the realization of Awakening "a." Practitioners center effort on becoming and remaining conscious of the causes and operation of conditioned states. Next, they learn how to cope with the dynamics of conditioned states without allowing the negative emotions that are associated with them to be projected onto the world. Learning to internally cope with conditioned states builds the creative tension that eventually brings about Awakening "A."

2. Separation

Separation is the first step of Zazen practice, wherein the arising of the continuous flow of mental, emotional, and physical events is observed. An observational viewpoint is gained through Zen training. In Zazen, one gains the ability to witness conditioned states and inquire into their function. The first effect of this observational and questioning attitude is that it provides a space between conditioned states and any habitual thought and emotional responses associated with them. Prior to establishing this mental and emotional distance, whatever is felt at any given moment is projected onto the external world. Negative emotions aroused by conditioned states are often automatically expressed. One becomes a victim of unawareness.

Dōgen's term for gaining this observational space is "not-thinking." "Not-thinking" does not mean suppressing thoughts and emotions. A steadfast nonjudgmental awareness observes their arising and falling without forming preferences about them. Being able to witness an object or event without preferences, without a desire to hold or push them away, creates the correct orientation.[6] The proper perspective of what to do—when to go forward and when to hold back—is the nuts and bolts of an unsullied orientation. Tung-shan, the founder of Soto Zen, described this attitude of mind in the *Song of the Jewel Mirror Awareness* as, "Turning away and touching are both wrong."[7] The impermanent nature of thoughts and emotions becomes apparent, establishing the basis for how to put Tung-shan's instruction into practice. Furthermore the value judgments habitually placed on thoughts and emotions are seen as tentative definitions, ultimately not good or bad, they just are. This is different from "they just are" as it is encountered in Identification because the conclusion comes from a conscious realization that minimizes or altogether removes the valuation. It does not derive from an unexamined assumption.

Not getting caught up in useless and injurious partialities, allows the practitioner to recognize the activities of the Universal aspect of the self. This new Universal perspective, depicted in the Nonduality Symbol as Awakening "a," evolves from the practice of Zazen and the introspection of Separation. This Universal perspective grows and manifests within the normal occurrences of daily life. It views life as intimately interconnected without any enduring component. Along with one's growing awareness of the Universal, the complementary "foci" relationship of the Universal with the Personal begins to have an influential effect on one's inner orientation toward the conditioned states, and their manifestation in outward behavior.

The individual's movement from Identification to Separation begins the process of conscious inquiry as the central point of Zen practice. Observation and inquiry are cultivated together and can be considered learning how to break the 2nd link of the Twelve Links of the Chain of Causation. Embodiment of observation and inquiry is a revolution of mind when compared to the unquestioning perspective of Identification. Separation uncovers the fundamental point of Buddhist practice—that Emptiness is the preeminent cure for the pain produced by the action of conditioned states.

3. Development

Within Development, the individual differentiates and closely examines the observational viewpoint. This is where conditioned states begin to deconstruct. The connection between negative emotions, mental pain, and conditioned states becomes apparent. The nature of their relationship is looked at in a broader sense with the observational awareness of Zazen practice.

Establishing a spiritual practice requires a foundation built on living a full and complete life. When embarking upon a spiritual quest, one adds that responsibility to the others already in place. John Welwood, in his book *Toward a Psychology of Awakening*, examines how people who seek awakening sometimes attempt to sidestep the difficulties of the worldly life by assuming spiritual insight, alone, will solve all their problems. Welwood calls this misguided effort "spiritual bypassing."[8] It is a common but mistaken response to the discomfort and dissatisfaction of life. In spiritual bypassing, problematic emotional and personal concerns are left unresolved, while one attempts spiritual practices as a means to find release from the afflictive emotions associated with personal issues.

Development is the opposite of spiritual bypassing. It recognizes and accepts duties as they come without shirking responsibility. It cooperates with the developmental process of maturity, responding with the Universal observational awareness the individual has met in the study of Separation. Deliberate and steadfast actions and an uncompromising introspection are the chief qualities of Development. Facing up to everything does not mean the imbalances will be settled, but doing so brings at least a chance for positive change. Ultimately, one cannot avoid addressing the unresolved concerns; if the imbalances are not dealt with directly, they will come in the back door, usually in chaotic and destructive forms.

A common instruction given to Zen students is to "be in the moment." The stage of Development inquires into the experiential meaning of this teaching. Generally speaking, the inquiry delves into balancing the interplay of the foci. For example, lay practitioners often comment on the lack of time they have to devote to Zen practice because of the unending and valid demands of family, job, life partner, and community. The Universal endeavor of Zen appears at odds with the personal requirements of day-to-day living. However, if one momentarily drops the underlying assumption of confrontation between the Personal and Universal, and replaces it with a view of complementary action, a good deal of unnecessary strife fades away. A new pathway opens. The supposed clash between the interests of the Personal and Universal loses its irksomeness, and becomes instead an intricate harmonious dance. Another aspect of Dōgen's "think of not-thinking" takes shape. The Personal "thinking" and the Universal "not-thinking" maintain their unique differences. However, their reciprocal and compatible interplay displays itself as the long-sought-for nonthinking—the wisdom mind of Nonduality. In the end, all dualisms can be approached in this manner. Two-sided items such as psychological and spiritual, mundane and sacred, delusion and enlightenment, reveal their ultimate oneness. Zen is not practiced to gain something, remove defilements, or attain perfection. It seeks to realize and creatively partake in the complementary activity of our inherently dualistic nature.

In Development, Tung-shan's definition of inquiry from the *Song of the Jewel Mirror Awareness* aids in understanding the nature of the interplay. He proclaims in that definition, "Subtly included within the true, inquiry and response come up together."[9] The "true" is ourselves, in the widest and most encompassing view of what constitutes the self. "Subtly" refers to the quiet, deep awareness cultivated in order to witness the operation of the "true" as it unfolds in our lives. "Inquiry and response come up together" is the tranquility of Zazen. Tranquility consists of a dynamic continuity of awareness, where awareness itself is inquiry, and insight the response. One establishes and cultivates the intimate relationship of inquiry and response within the ever-arising world of awakening.

Thus, our orientation toward conditioned states should not be hostile. Conditioned states are opportunities to advance spiritual insight. They are the gift that leads to liberation and the resolution that comes with our conscious participation in the interplay of the foci. They offer us the possibility of a life free of emotional bondage.

4. Maturation

In the preceding three stages of Identification, Separation, and Development, afflictive emotions were observed arising from the actions of conditioned states. Moving along the path of Deconstruction, our experience-based learning offers insights into deeper levels of their functioning and operation. Interdicting conditioned states as they arise is the way to break the 2nd Link in the Chain of Causation.

Maturation provides the practitioner with the inner firmness and strength required to recognize, accept, and keep the effects of conditioned states internalized. One observes their rise and fall with a minimal projection of negative responses into the world. Associated negative emotions are allowed to be what they are internally, but not expressed outwardly. Not projecting negative emotions generates creative tension that ultimately serves the process of their resolution. However, even with the conscious control of the effects of the conditioned states, one still experiences the pain of afflictive emotions. Maturation is not freedom from conditioned states. It is coping with the afflictive pain, but not the resolution of its root cause.

In Separation, the ability to observe and reflect on thinking with Dōgen's not-thinking promotes the awareness of the Universal aspect. One experiences and appreciates the Universal, but it plays a minor role in diminishing the effects of conditioned states. The influence of the latter continues to dominate the mental panorama. One of the most difficult turnabouts for practitioners to embody is to revere the "nonfabricated" voice of nature. It speaks clearly, but doubt as to its veracity lies deep within the skepticism of Western minds. In Maturation, the tables are turned. Now the Universal becomes powerful enough to permit the practitioner to use its positive and thoroughgoing vision to overcome the mistrust. This strong Universal perspective allows a vigorous and close examination of conditioned states without getting trapped by them. Their harmful effects are not quite put to rest, yet they are, for the most part recognized for what they are and dealt with appropriately.

In Maturation, the elements of Buddhist faith—trust and confidence—emerge from the practitioner confirming the truth of the inherent nondual voice of *Buddhanature*. The habitual skepticism that normally surrounds the genuineness of this voice lessens as erroneous views loosen their grip. One of the most difficult tasks is trusting the source and content of information that resides at the center of authentic practice. The beneficent activity of the universe lies beyond doubt within an accepting trust, one based on experiential understanding, not beliefs. Trust and confidence are essential to making progress, as they are the heart of Buddhist awakening.

5. Transformation

Transformation is Awakening "A," a life-determining event that results from efforts in study, introspection, and Zazen. Transformation is a breakthrough to a change of being wherein the voice of the *Buddhadharma* sounds clear and keen. Within this creative action, the conditioned state and its related afflictive pain are resolved. The pain changes from a symptomatic issue to productive energy and insight. With the obstacle removed, coping is not necessary because the afflictive outcome of the conditioned state is no longer present. In resolution, the psychophysical formation within which the conditioned state is rooted disintegrates, and the mind and body are free from its influences. This is the foundation of Buddhist liberation.

Transformation is a sudden event, one that arrives fully formed within consciousness, along with a sense of certainty and joyful rapport. It is an intuition of something new, an outcome of an inquiry whose immediate response answers with complete appropriateness the practitioner's idiosyncratic Natural Koan. The sudden breakthrough to clarity, however, is not without antecedent struggle. A great deal of time most often precedes the unexpected conclusion. In Zen, this is known as gradual practice. The sudden breakthrough would not have occurred without continuing efforts over a long period. Nonetheless, the gradual effort does not itself bring about the sudden breakthrough. The "sudden" and "gradual" interact as foci, not as elements in a causal relationship, nor opposites that somehow have to be merged together. Rather, they maintain their individuality and differences, as well as their intimate involvement. Their relationship is one of complementary activity, within which Nonduality abides.

Gradual practice is essential to develop a strong foundation, and it is also necessary afterwards to sustain and cultivate the beneficial effects of the breakthrough. Dōgen's teaching of practice/realization maintains this pattern of interconnection of dualistic elements. Other pairs such as Personal and Universal, form and Emptiness, delusion and enlightenment, mind and body, and an endless string of others find their relationship defined and expressed within the same dynamic interchange.

Transformation and its concurrent advent of freedom establish an open and intimate relationship to one's life. This openness arises from an expanded comprehension of the hallmarks of Mahayana Buddhism: the all-encompassing wisdom of Emptiness, the recognition of the interdependence of all beings, and the acknowledgment that all phenomena express Universal truth.

6. Psychophysical Shift

A Psychophysical Shift signifies the completion of Deconstruction. After a breakthrough occurs and a conditioned state is resolved, one needs to critically evaluate the changes that have taken place. The Psychophysical Shift unburdens the practitioner of the mental habits and deep-seated assumptions embedded in the conditioned state. Without their encumbrance, an individual's experience of self is radically altered. An entirely new point of reference replaces that which was formally taken as normal, predictable, and essential. Freedom from the aspects of alienation and separation—the product of the fundamental misperception—becomes the heart of the self. Physical and mental constraints are replaced with feelings of release, openness, and relaxation. Discomfort associated with the transformed conditioned state recedes. One may experience a perceptual disorientation arising from being free of problematic symptoms that at one time seemed to be integral and inseparable from one's self. Emotional infatuation with feelings of liberation may also occur for a brief period of time.

Conditioned states are rooted in psychophysical formations within the body. These formations are brought into being by actions in this life, or inherited from an individual's physical or spiritual ancestors. "This life" formations are the outcome of an individual's personal experience; whereas inherited formations are the totality of one's inborn tendencies, the focus of the Universal conditioning in a person's life. The breakthrough of Transformation dissolves the psychophysically embedded formation. Prior to this, coping with the attendant afflictive emotions was the best that could be done. Afterwards, the physical and mental landscape is free of the pain that arose when the conditioned state was triggered. The healing process is one that is beyond willful volition. It is impossible to resolve conditioned states by just thinking about them. Only a holistic methodology that brings about Transformation can yield a complete solution. The combination of introspection and Zazen provides the means to plumb the depths of conditioned states, see what they really are, and establish the circumstances for their elimination.

The Resolution Sequence deals with both the Personal and Universal types of psychophysical formations. Which formation is resolved in Transformation depends on one's center of attention during the stages of Identification through Maturation. During the process building up to Transformation, one develops an expanding inner awareness of the unique psychophysical geography underlying a conditioned state. It will have a very specific location. Conditioned states manifest in many different forms that vary with each individual for each problem.

The originating cause of the Personal psychophysical formations is more easily understood than what causes the Universal type. Such formations originate from negative circumstances, as the individual subjectively experiences them, and how the experience is stored as a symptom in the body. These Personal psychophysical formations are a complex matrix of thoughts and emotions. The cause of the Universal formations is not as obvious because they are not just a product of an individual's life history, but come from the complex web that underlies every being's existence. [See Sandy's story in Chapter 4] Most often, successful resolution of the Universal formations requires that the Personal ones be addressed and resolved first. This establishes a firm foundation for future attention on the Universal aspects.

Reconstruction – The Study of the Integration of Freedom

Reconstruction is similar to the progression of the stages in Deconstruction. In Deconstruction, knowledge of the existence of conditioned states emerges, then one attains understanding of the nature of their influence, and finally one achieves the conscious will to internalize the negative emotions. It is this internalization that eventually brings about Transformation. Reconstruction is concerned with integrating freedom and eliminating the vestigial effects of the uprooted conditioned state. Integration establishes and cultivates the practitioner's activities of body, speech, and thought so they accord with the voice of the *Buddhadharma*.

Reconstruction is learning to live the freedom garnered in Transformation, thus integrating the change of being realized in Awakening "A." Reconstruction establishes a new morality based on a transformed state of being. The entire process of Reconstruction can be considered a conscious cultivation and integration of the vision and freedom of Awakening "A." Reconstruction deals with liberation—the unimpeded activity of the foci of the Personal and Universal aspects of being. It offers a means by which the emerging experience of freedom can mature and be integrated into all aspects of life. Reconstruction acknowledges the preeminent capability of freedom and the wisdom of Emptiness as its unifying force, granting language, reason, creativity, human sentiment, and ethical relations their proper and deserved places as integration proceeds.

The Six Stages of Reconstruction

7. Proclamation

Proclamation begins the process of Reconstruction. The term Proclamation captures the content of the moment: the change issued through Transformation announces that the old way of being has passed, and that now a new spiritual dimension animates the core of one's efforts. An abiding sense of accomplishment penetrates one's practice and relieves mental obscurations of their central place. It proclaims freedom from the tyranny of the afflictive emotions connected with a conditioned state. One gains the capability to recognize, accept, and take joy in the release from a habitual dynamic. Freedom from the pain of afflictive emotions becomes the norm. This in itself is quite agreeable and beneficial. Proclamation is the full opening of the Universal, the pivot point of the changeover from concentration on a conditioned state to living the truth of freedom.

Transformation eradicates both physical and mental obstacles. Francesca Fremantle describes eradication this way: "[In Buddhism] liberation is not *of* the self, but *from* the self."[10] Before its resolution, one could only imagine what life would be like without the influence of the conditioned state. In some ways, its influence was even considered essential to one's sense of self. Now the conditioned state, and all that issued from it are understood to have been a barrier to liberation. Resolving the root of the conditioned state opens new opportunities for deepening Zazen practice. Prior to Transformation, a lot of attention and effort is required to keep the damaging effects of the conditioned state from escaping into the world. That requirement is no longer necessary. The practitioner experiences exhilaration arising from the recognition of the extent and enduring character of the changes brought on by Transformation.

Even though the wisdom of the Universal governs the mental landscape, leftover habit energies of the resolved conditioned state may occasionally still be felt. However, they no longer dominate as before because Transformation has freed the practitioner from the habitual response.

* * *

The next three stages of Discerning Differences, Clarifying Details, and Acceptance are experienced within the Meditative Landscape. The practitioner centers effort on becoming conscious of the new responses, and how to integrate the freedom they bring into daily life. This phase of the process is Awakening "Aa." One must consciously cultivate the change of being, with its allied sense of freedom first encountered in Transformation, in order to produce the energy level required to bring about Awakening "AA." Awakening "Aa" rejoins the enhanced Universal of the stages of Transformation, Psychophysical Shift, and Proclamation with the Personal side now open to change. Their interplay is one of joy and insight. Freedom is not just a state of mind, but also the wherewithal to respond to the needs of others. Creative contributions to the well-being of the community are its spontaneous effects.

8. Discerning Differences

Discerning Differences is Awakening "Aa" wherein the practitioner closely regards the functioning of the freedom attained in Awakening "A." One discerns the different states of being, before and after Transformation, and notes their distinguishing features. In the stage of Separation, Awakening "a," a new perspective results from observing the emotional bondage caused by unresolved conditioned states. In Discerning Differences, one cultivates another new perspective, that of monitoring freedom from affliction. A special effort is required to make the operation of the differences conscious, and to avoid naïve understanding. It is important to observe the differences closely for an extended period in order to solidify the favorable results, and to reduce the tendency to take the new life situation for granted.

Awareness of the differences enhances the effects of the psychophysical shift. Because what we used to cling to is no longer present, a certain amount of disorientation is inevitable. Closely examining the significant changes tends to minimize the disorientation. One can observe the differences brought about by the psychophysical shift, and even scrutinize any disorientation, because of the strength of the new internal environment.

The practitioner also examines the connection between psychophysical shift and freedom from afflictive pain. When the physical or mental remnants of the conditioned state appear, they are experienced as rootless and ephemeral. These habitual patterns associated with the conditioned states no longer have the power to cause afflictive responses. They present themselves, drawing attention, but without influence or control. The control now resides in one's burgeoning knowledge and ability to take whatever influences the habit energies have left and transform them into an even greater amount of perceptual and behavioral freedom.

9. Clarifying Details

In Clarifying Details, the practitioner clearly articulates observed differences, appreciating and enjoying them as freedom, while drawing upon them for reflection. Conscious cultivation of the new freedom brings about increased comfort levels, and one is less prone to drop into an unsophisticated understanding that can induce a premature sense of satisfaction. One experiences the differences as more and more commonplace, yet Reconstruction is incomplete, and effort must be continued. The novelty of Transformation recedes into the background, as freedom becomes the normal way of sensing the self. The residue of the resolved conditioned state is more easily dealt with. Now only minimal effort is required to dismiss the rootless and powerless tendencies connected with it. At this stage, one no longer mistrusts intuitive knowledge. Instead, the mind-set of freedom unifies itself with the constructive information that wells up in Zazen.

In Development, one establishes the observational and questioning viewpoint as the everyday attitude of mind; in Clarifying Details, cultivation of the everyday mind holds the highest importance for oneself and others. Relief from habitual painful distractions opens new vistas. One now perceives the dualistic foci of Personal and Universal to be alive and actively embodied as a radiant light. This light does not transform our dualistic makeup into some vague oneness, but rather brings about a firm understanding of how the foci are, and always have been, a creative complement.

10. Acceptance

Acceptance is grounded in the practitioner's trust and confidence in the validity and durability of the changes experienced. One can fully grasp the significance of the transition from the problematic symptom, but effort is still required to recognize the differences. Perceiving the depth of the changes brings an enhanced sense of satisfaction, pleasure, and gratitude. It is understandable to want to stay at this stage because it is so pleasant, but another leap is necessary, and that leap grows out of an energetic and directed vision.

The *Brahma Viharas*[11], the pure abodes of Buddhism, arise and mature during the process of awakening, growing out of acquired wisdom and authentic practice. They are expressions of the Buddhist freedom of Awakening "A."

Brahma Viharas	**Personal Attribute**	**Universal Attribute**
Kindness: Making room for others	Healing	Connection
Compassion: Embracing self and others	Forgiveness/Repentance	Harmony
Sympathetic Joy: Concept of self separate from other vanishes	Nonspecific gratitude	Interdependence
Acceptance: Unencumbered activity of no self-nature	Equanimity	Intimacy

The *Brahma Viharas* express themselves in small and grand ways. Zen practice and the Reconstruction portion of the Resolution Sequence unbundle constraints, one by one, and occasionally in clusters. Each release, however tiny, has a transforming effect on the personality of the individual expressed through action, speech, and thought. The Personal attributes act internally and in one-to-one encounters. The Universal attributes draw us into Indra's Net[12], the place of intimacy with the world that is release from the fundamental misperception. As Francis Cook reflects, dwelling in Indra's Net transports us to the end of self-indulgence:

> When in a rare moment I manage painfully to rise above the petty individualism by knowing my true nature, I perceive I dwell in the wondrous net of Indra, and in this incredible network of interdependence, the career of the Bodhisattva must begin. It is not just that 'we are in it' together. We are it, rising or falling as one living body.[13]

11. Relief and Comfort

During Separation, a new intention powered by a glimmer of truth, sets the stage for an adventure, wherein one seeks the mind of freedom beyond William Blake's "mind-forged manacles." A new direction shows itself and eventually leads to Relief and Comfort. The fundamental misperception of the tendency to reify the self drops away.

Awakening "AA" is the culmination of the path to Buddhist liberation, where unity is attained. Relief and Comfort is a *breakthrough to a change of behavior*. A breakthrough arises when it will, growing out of the deep penetration into Discerning

Differences, Clarifying Details, and Acceptance. The habit energies no longer come up; consequently effort is no longer needed to cultivate the vision of Awakening "A" because its positive influences have been fully integrated. One's freedom is expressed in healing old wounds, harmonious relations, and nonspecific gratitude, as well as in one's spontaneous enjoyment of life. A young Zen priest was once asked, "How do Buddhists do away with desire?" Before the priest could respond the questioner answered his own inquiry with, "They already have everything they want: contentment." Contentment, peace, and joy are indeed the hallmarks of a life imbued with Awakening "AA." Contentment can be regarded as the fifth *Brahma Vihara.*

The individual who attains Awakening "AA" relates to the world fully in both its Personal and Universal aspects. Deconstruction focused on acquiring Universal truth in order to reduce, and ultimately resolve, the illusionary veil brought on by the functioning of conditioned states. Reconstruction established the concordant activity of Personal truth with the Universal. Without the Personal, the Universal remains apart from the world, and the visionary elements of Awakening "A" are never fully incorporated into one's life. The Personal and Universal aspects work as harmonious foci to generate the energy of the transformative shift of Relief and Comfort.

12. Naturalness

Accomplishing Awakening "AA" allows one to live effortlessly and unselfconsciously, freed from previous restrictions. Naturalness is activated awareness, with Unencumbered Activity the effortless outcome. With complete integration of the changes rendered through Transformation, no notions of the Personal and Universal aspects remain.

The mind of Naturalness includes all beings. With nothing excluded, turning a blind eye to immediate and far-reaching relationships is impossible. The large, generous, compassionate, and sharing mind of Naturalness responds with indiscriminate goodwill. "We go up to the mountain for ourselves; we come down from the mountain for others."[14] Deconstruction of the conditioned state is going up; Reconstruction is coming down. In the Genjo Koan, Dōgen insists that enlightenment exists when the self is perfectly pervious to the myriad beings and events of the world. Delusion insists that the world match the needs of an individual's assumptions; awakening opens the self to the free activity of all beings. The self and the world maintain their identities yet "…the true inside of the inside is not having an inside or outside."[15]

The Resolution Sequence follows the path of introspection and awakening from the unawareness of Identification to the wholeness of Naturalness. This process results in the freedom of Unencumbered Activity, the mind of contented ordinariness, as the bottom leg of the triangle indicates. Completion of one circle prepares one for further work on the path. Numerous trips around the triangle are necessary.

Zazen – Introspection

The Nonduality – Resolution Sequence lays out a means of inquiry that permits empirical knowledge gained in the awakening process to be as unbounded as possible by any a priori theory or expectation. This is especially true for what is gained in Transformation and Relief and Comfort, where altogether new and unexpected breakthroughs occur. Aside from sudden awakenings, the stages flow from one to another without sharp distinction. Insight into the meaning of a particular stage automatically engages the subsequent stage. An example of this movement can be recognized in Identification, when one is able to articulate the previously unconscious issue. This conscious observation provides distance from the issue, the beginning of Separation. Similarly, when the observation of Separation deepens to the point where one understands how the conditioned state operates, Development begins as the root of condition state begins to deconstruct.

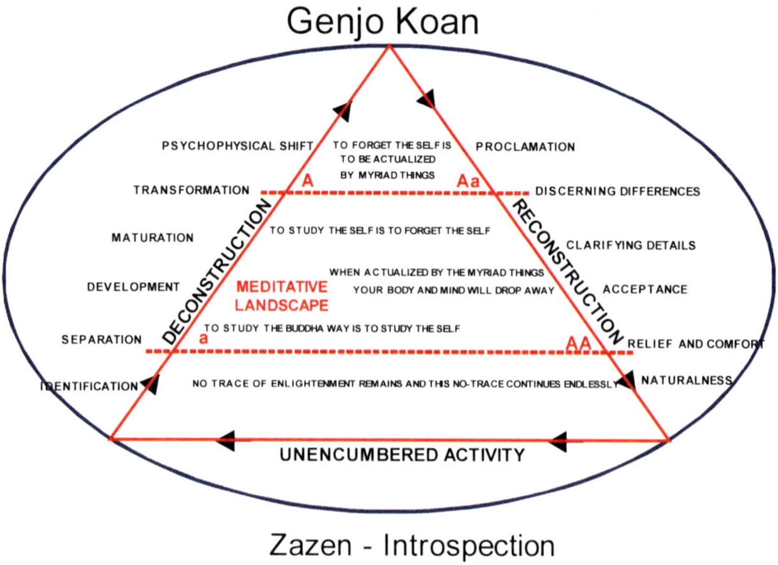

FIGURE 3

The combination of Nonduality and the Resolution Sequence yields an introspective guide. This guide by itself provides an exceedingly practical foundation upon which a lifetime of inquiry into the nature of reality can be erected. Additionally, as we will see in the next chapters, it offers other methods of approaching Zen study.

An example of this method would be placing Dōgen's famous five-statement passage on the self from the Genjo Koan on the Nonduality-Resolution Sequence Symbol.

> To study the Buddha Way is to study the self. To study the self is to forget the self. To forget the self is to be actualized by myriad things. When actualized by the myriad things, your body and mind as well as the bodies and minds of others drop away. No trace of enlightenment remains, and this no-trace continues endlessly.[16]

Doing so, unveils how the combination of the five statements and symbol offers a broadened understanding of Dogen's introspective intent. He insists that practitioners undertake a thoroughgoing introspection of the self in order to overturn deeply entrenched assumptions. These five statements, combined with the Nonduality – Resolution Sequence Symbol, demonstrate how this symbol can be used to structure the study and practice of Buddhist teachings. The following is a brief analysis of the Genjo Koan's five statements when viewed through the lens of the Nonduality – Resolution Sequence Symbol.

To study the Buddha Way is to study the self.

The above statement can be understood as Identification and Separation, where the Universal starts to act within one's life. Zazen is Dōgen's *study*. It is the beginning of Awakening "a." Zazen provides the ability to observe the self in action, and to describe the self's makeup and operation.

To study the self is to forget the self.

This statement reflects Development and Maturation, the full flowering of Awakening "a," where the Universal [conscious observation and questioning] is large in proportion to the Personal. *To forget the self* happens naturally when we learn to see the world in another way: conditioned states are embraced and afflictive emotions associated with them are not projected on the world.

To forget the self is to be actualized by myriad things.

This is Transformation, Psychophysical Shift, and Proclamation: Awakening "A." A new worldview spreads out and invites one to look deeply. The Universal dominates because a Transformation has taken place, removing the conditioned barriers, and the *myriad things* manifest within an individual. A psychophysical shift has occurred. While attempting to make the world conform to the self is hopeless, painful, and disappointing, opening fully to the *myriad things* is fulfilling, stimulating, and satisfying.

When actualized by the myriad things, your body and mind as well as the bodies and minds of others will drop away.
"Body and mind … will drop away" is Discerning Differences, Clarifying Details, and Acceptance—Awakening "Aa"—where the freedom of Reconstruction replaces the conditioning of Deconstruction. The *myriad things* of the Universal act in complementary accord with the re-emerging Personal, refining the intellect, emotions, speech, reason, intuition, and form. The outcome is a balanced and happy person.

No trace of enlightenment remains and this no-trace continues endlessly.
This is Relief and Comfort and Naturalness of Awakening "AA"—perpetual awakening. Effortless living is at the heart of *no-trace* realization. *No-trace* means one fully engages the world unself-consciously.

Summary of the Resolution Sequence

The table below is a shorthand summary of the Resolution Sequence stages. It is a simplified guide and a one-word definition for each part of the process.

Deconstruction	Reconstruction
1. Identification – Articulating	7. Proclamation – Asserting
2. Separation – Observing	8. Discerning Differences – Noting
3. Development – Questioning	9. Clarifying Details – Opening
4. Maturation – Embracing	10. Acceptance – Having
5. Transformation – Liberating	11. Relief and Comfort – Being
6. Psychophysical Shift – Losing	12. Naturalness – Sharing

Chapter 4
THE NATURAL KOAN

Chapter 2, Nonduality, introduced the basics of Dōgen's Zen: practice-centered, experiential wisdom focused on dynamic movement, and the interplay of the foci of the Personal and Universal aspects of being. Chapter 3, The Nonduality – Resolution Sequence, defined an introspective method that instructs how to work with conditioned states in Deconstruction, and the successful integration of earned freedom through Reconstruction. Figure 4, The Natural Koan Symbol, demonstrates how this movement is accomplished.

Figure 3, The Nonduality – Resolution Sequence Symbol, is modified with the three elements of the Natural Koan: Conditioned States, Inquiry, and Breakthrough. Conditioned States are set in the lower portion of the triangle next to Identification. This indicates that they shape behavior with a minimum of conscious understanding as to their pervasive influence. Inquiry functions within the Meditative Landscape of Separation, Development, and Maturation, the area where one becomes conscious of conditioned state dynamics in Deconstruction; and Discerning Differences, Clarifying Details, and Acceptance is where one integrates freedom in Reconstruction. Breakthrough is in the area of Transformation, Psychophysical Shift, and Proclamation, where the practitioner first attains resolution/freedom. The combined elements are the Natural Koan itself.

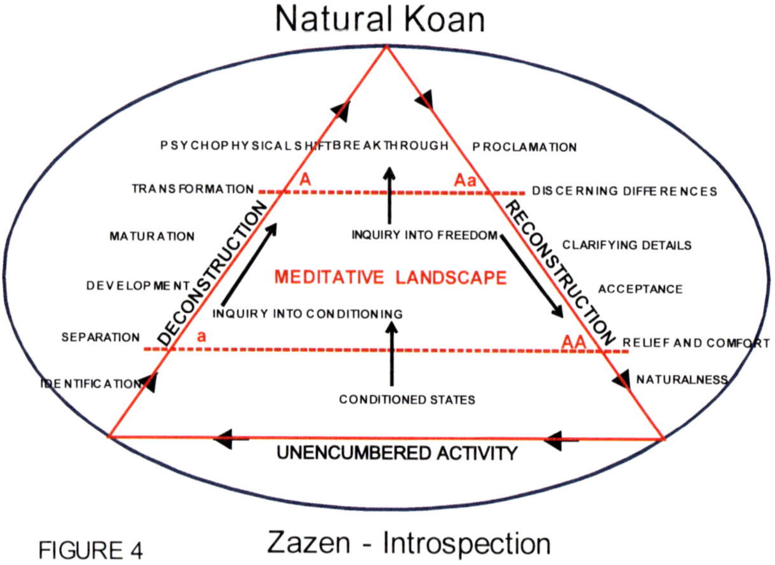

FIGURE 4

The Natural Koan

The form of the Natural Koan[17] is the essential, original, and creative root into the inquiry of the nature of self. This inquiry focuses on the fundamental misperception of a practitioner's sense of separation from the world. The Natural Koan is a personal, idiosyncratic expression of this Universal issue that at first manifests as a barrier but which, with practice, is transformed into the living Dharma. Before undertaking conscious work with one's Natural Koan, the negative emotional charge embedded in conditioned states reigns supreme. It is termed "natural" because awareness of its makeup is innate to an individual, not something fabricated or taken on. One's central issue arises and is distilled within the sphere of a penetrating spiritual inquiry.

The Natural Koan's overarching theme, and the tension it produces, has been likened to a fish with a hot iron ball in its mouth that it could neither swallow nor spit out. Faced with a dilemma of that magnitude it behooves one to work diligently toward one's freedom. Both the obstructions to progress and the means to resolve them are contained within the Natural Koan. Asking questions and learning to trust the responses that arise from the depths of one's being refine the understanding and functioning of the Natural Koan. Trust and confidence in the process grow with self-observation of how the Natural Koan operates in one's life.

The Natural Koan offers amplification of the meaning of the previously discussed Zen instruction to "be in the moment." Zen teachers repeat this statement often so that their students gain a comprehensive awareness of their personal set of conditions. The simplicity and potent depth of that teaching acts as a touchstone for Zen practice. The Natural Koan engages a number of questions that evolve out of this instruction, such as, "What is a moment?" and "What does it mean to be in the moment?" Further inquiries lead to questioning what to do with the knowledge gained by asking such questions. Zazen, and the introspective power of the

Resolution Sequence, successfully ask and answer these questions, and others comparable to them.

In today's world, the intimate life of master and disciple that served as the vehicle for resolution is a rare event for the modern Zen practitioner. It appears that the busy life of the layperson would negate the possibility of placing this type of inquiry at the center of one's spiritual endeavor. However, the central issue of the Natural Koan still arises and can coalesce out of a questioning mindset whatever the life circumstance of the individual.

The Natural Koan is closely akin to the inquiry of the ancient Chinese Zen monk. However, a layperson's Natural Koan can be many-sided because of the number of different roles he or she is expected to perform. Monks in a monastery discover and refine their Natural Koan quickly because a monastic life offers limited distractions. Lay practitioners must polish their knowledge and understanding of their spiritual question within the rapid-fire existence of modern life. The master-monk relationships of old are replaced with daily encounters that ignite difficulties or spark insights, both of which emanate from the Natural Koan. Nevertheless, the goal is the same. No matter what the circumstance, all Zen students, monk or lay, are attempting the same thing: to awaken in themselves the experiential insights that the Buddha attained.

Examples of Natural Koans

There are many examples of Natural Koans in the Zen record from ancient times. Below are three familiar accounts that demonstrate the range of questions raised that can serve as the distillation of an individual's existential dilemma. The Natural Koan is a call to action. Once it arises, it engenders an intense questioning that, if followed, produces the energy for breakthrough.

It seems only proper to begin with the Buddha. Shakyamuni Buddha's Natural Koan emerged from his encounter with the sick, elderly, and deceased. Over time, his question formulated itself: "Why is there suffering in the world?" The form of the inquiry reflects how deeply compassion had already penetrated him. Buddha did not ask, "Why am I suffering?" His devotion was dedicated to solving the issue for all beings.

The second example is from the record of Zen Master Tung-shan. His Natural Koan first exhibited itself when he was quite young. He heard that the National Teacher of China maintained that everything in the world, including such things as rocks, mountains, and rivers, constantly proclaim the Dharma. This statement raised questions for Tung-shan that eventually coalesced as, "How do insentient beings preach the Dharma?"

Lastly, we have the spiritual quandary of Zen Master Dōgen. "If we are already Buddha, why do we have to practice?"

These three examples clearly demonstrate how an individual's personal spiritual dilemma operates as a powerful force in the awakening process.

Conditioned States

Conditioned states manifest as a continuous stream of habitual responses to environmental causes. These causes can be either external events or internal stimuli. They express themselves automatically with negative emotional tones that are often considered "normal," because they have existed within us for most or all of our conscious life. Conditioned states leave a painful wake, one of reactive response and disharmony. No amount of well-intended willful action seems to have any permanent effect at alleviating its dynamics, let alone its root cause. Understanding what conditioned states are helps in forming a correct view of our existential dilemma. Without a correct view, Zen practice has a shaky foundation. With intellectual knowledge and firsthand experience about the form and function of conditioned states, Zen practice becomes infused with energy and direction. Conditioned states are transformed in Zazen – Introspection, where their toxic activity is converted into a healing remedy.

Early twentieth century author, Lafcadio Hearn, recounts a fragment of a Japanese tale that gives force to the intensity of scrutiny one must apply to conditioned states in order to grasp the depth of their penetration into human life. In the tale, a Bodhisattva is leading a seeker up a mountain with the summit far away and lost in a moonless gloom. The Bodhisattva offers assurances to his companion, "What you have asked to see will be shown to you. But the place of Vision is far; and the way is rude. Follow after me, and do not fear: strength will be given you."[18]

So the two tread wearily upward, sometimes dislodging unseen masses that roll down the mountainside with a hollow clatter. They climb through the night with only an occasional pinpoint of starlight as their beacon. The seeker struggles mightily, expending more-than-human effort inspired by the supportive coaxing of the Bodhisattva.

As the dawn approaches, the weary seeker at last recognizes on what he has been climbing. "I fear!—unutterably I fear … there is nothing but the skulls of men!" "A mountain of skulls it is," responded the Bodhisattva. "But know my son, that all of them are your own! Each has at some time been the nest of your dreams and delusions and desires. Not even one of them is the skull of another being. All—without exception—have been yours, in the billions of your former lives."[19]

The Bodhisattva's last statement brings to mind William Faulkner's famous assertion: "The past is never dead; it's not even past." The tale exemplifies every phenomenon, including each human life, has its origin deeply rooted in antiquity. It is impossible to locate a beginning or first cause. In regard to human life, every conditioned state has a cause that can be traced back to another, and that one, in turn, to another, until a mountain of skulls lies unnoticed beneath the veneer of our "ordinary" existence. This mountain of conditioned states is the product of lifetimes of unresolved grief.

Not only is the mountain of conditioned states ancient, it is vast as well. Within us, a multitude of such states, manifesting with infinite variation in response to myriad triggers, forms a web of unimaginable complexity. And this "cosmic soup" is where we live.

One practitioner we know, whom we will call "Sandy," related the following personal experience with a dislodged skull from her mountain. Sandy was in her mid-twenties when her life was suddenly overturned by the premonition she would die by a shot to the back of her head. "That's how I experienced this knowing of what it is like to wait to be executed. That it was something that was going to happen." Sandy related that she had no sense of when this might occur. As difficult as this knowing was, there were times when she had a neutral response to it. There were even times when she was able to support some doubt about this intrusive knowing.

Then things intensified. At unpredictable times, she would become overwhelmed with the feeling that it was going to happen now! She could be walking down a street or sitting on a bus, not remotely thinking about being shot, and the next moment experience a sense of panic because the event felt imminent. Sandy couldn't help but think she was going crazy. "Why am I so paranoid, all of a sudden?"

Sandy was also confused by the particularity of the event. She did not experience a generalized fear of being harmed in multiple ways, or have excessive anxiety about other things. Her fear was specific to being shot in the back of the head. She could not relate to what was happening. These "paranoid episodes," as she referred to them, increased with intensity and frequency until she could no longer dismiss what was happening.

She sought counseling. However, discussing the problem did nothing to alleviate it. Stress reduction techniques also proved inadequate. Although she used anti-anxiety medication a few times with some effect, it was not a satisfying answer to "why" this was happening, nor a remedy she wanted to depend on.

Sandy had been a Zen practitioner for a number of years. Finally she got up the nerve to discuss what was happening with her teacher. Because these episodes made her feel crazy, she feared that if she told others her experience they would think she was crazy, too. During a private interview with her teacher she asked, "How do you explain knowing things that can't be related to any experience you've had in your life?"

Her teacher asked if she had an example. This was the moment she dreaded, but Sandy plunged ahead. "How do you explain that I know exactly what it feels like to wait to be shot in the back of the head, when of course, I've never experienced that?"

Without hesitation her teacher replied, "That's how we smell our past lives."

Whoa! That was an answer she did not see coming. What a jolting shock! Sandy explained that she had been what she now calls, "an existential Zen practitioner." Yes, she had benefited from the meditation, attended dharma talks, and did some reading, but she hadn't yet delved into the deeper aspects of Buddhist teachings, such as karma or rebirth. Now, here was a man she respected very much telling her, "That's how we smell our past lives."

For the first time since the whole problem began, she had to consider that maybe it wasn't something about to happen, but was instead a memory of something that had already occurred. Not that this was any explanation that resolved the mystery. And why "smell" our past lives? But the effect of that comment over time was to give Sandy the ability to better manage the episodes. They became less frequent and less intense.

Nevertheless, it was several more years before the whole dynamic resolved. The turning point came when Sandy experienced a spiritual crisis, accompanied by a near-fatal physical illness. All the intense pain from that illness was referred to the back of her head, at the precise spot where she had anticipated being shot. Working through her spiritual crisis and illness resulted in the total resolution of the problem."[20]

Sandy's story is certainly intriguing. Generally speaking, people accept that we have a physical inheritance. We are told we have Grandma's eyes or Dad's height. We even accept that we have family traits of behavior or mannerisms. But if it is suggested that our psyches are not ours alone, there is vociferous resistance to the notion. This is yet another way we are attached to the idea of a "separate" self.

The number of different attitudes toward conditioned states appears to be as abundant as the massive amount of conditioned states themselves. Standpoints vary from ignorance of them to believing that one cannot really change. *That's just the way I am.* Other orientations include the lack of skill in relating to them, or trying to think one's way out of their effects. Becoming satisfied with coping strategies is one of the subtlest confinements that can entrap an individual. While creative and patient coping with conditioned states can greatly improve our lives, it is only in Transformation that we attain resolution.

Inquiry

On the Natural Koan Symbol, Inquiry within the Meditative Landscape is defined in two ways: Inquiry into Conditioned States, and Inquiry into Freedom. Inquiry into conditioned states is the movement toward the Universal aspect of being that first appeared in Separation, where one becomes conscious of the detrimental effects of a conditioned state. The influence of the Universal grows within Deconstruction, coming to full force in the breakthrough of Transformation. Via the Inquiry into Freedom, the practitioner is able to integrate the Universal with the Personal in Reconstruction, achieving their full accord with the second breakthrough of Relief and Comfort.

The Meditative Landscape of the Natural Koan is termed Inquiry for both Deconstruction and Reconstruction because Inquiry is the very essence of Zen practice. An individual's Natural Koan becomes known and provides the continuity of awareness in Deconstruction necessary for Transformation. Then, Reconstruction provides guidance for the successful integration of the newly gained freedom. Inquiry is a matter beyond mere curious dabbling, however, Inquiry founded on Zazen – Introspection demands commitment of the highest order. Only a practitioner's purposeful and dedicated engagement with continuous inner dialogue has the requisite meaningful force to carry one through to Transformation. Inquiry into what constitutes a conditioned state begins the long struggle to undermine the fixed notions of self, and leads to an intimate and liberated way of living beyond them.

Inquiry into conditioned states begins and deepens the inner dialogue. It establishes observation and questioning as the chief means of gathering experiential evidence on which to base one's life. Acquiring conscious knowledge of our conditioning provides the basis for understanding how the will can be applied to engender and enhance inner strength. Ironically, it takes a healthy sense of self to approach the liberating experience of no self-nature. Ultimately, inquiry leads to consideration of the fundamental tenet of Buddhist psychology—that the self is essentially transitory, and that the notion of a permanent and fixed self is without basis. This realization places the practitioner on top of the hundred-foot pole to ask: "What happens next?"

Inquiry into Freedom occurs after the breakthrough of Transformation. Here the Universal, which one has sought and found in the breakthrough, begins to act in accord with the Personal. The practitioner now cultivates and values all of the skills put into the service of achieving breakthrough as a means to serve the community at large. Thinking, language, artistic expression, social graces, and intuition are refined by their creative interaction with the Universal. One's concept of self and other diminishes as the vision of indivisibility and interdependence becomes prominent. Residual habit energies appear from time to time but are not problematic. One no longer responds to them in the old way. Relief and Comfort removes the last vestige of habit energies and clears the way into Unencumbered Activity.

Engagement with both forms of Inquiry follows a general path that begins with personalizing the question at the heart of Zen practice, the form of one's Natural Koan. The question can be articulated and observed as it expresses itself in daily life. Gathering knowledge and familiarity over time, the inquiry broadens into a concise question that holds the individual's existential query, such as the Buddha's, "Why is there suffering in the world?" That question then resonates throughout the practitioner's activities. It develops a life of its own. And sometime, we don't know when, it delivers the liberating answer. This can be termed universalizing the Personal. Eventually the Universal view dominates and resolves the original existential question. Universal wisdom and one's unique personality then find the means to nurture each other, eventually giving rise to a complementary accord that requires no conscious intent.

Breakthrough

In ancient times when Zen practice was beginning in China, active exchanges took place between masters and disciples based on the close-knit relationship of their shared lives. Monks expressed their spiritual inquiry and doubt by posing questions, and masters responded with attempts to assist their "breakthrough" by action of a "turning word." Sometimes the turning word was enough to open a monk's mind, to take him beyond words and concepts, but oftentimes not. Even though the encounter took place within the world of language, it could bring forth a direct intuition of the Truth. This was breakthrough, the moment when the question posed in the Natural Koan resolved itself.[21]

Breakthroughs launch one into a new world where the stranglehold of the conditioned state, fervently studied and engaged with great energy, is suddenly and permanently uprooted. Such breakthroughs are sudden events; new information and vision "breaks" into consciousness. A strange and intriguing environment of vast openness and radiance presents itself. Former attitudes and conceptions of self, once considered essential, are no longer supported and disperse like smoke in a breeze. Afflictive emotions no longer dominate. There are large breakthroughs and small ones. They should be distinguished for what they are, and then, it is wise to move on quickly, as our attachment to the pleasant aspects of awakening is just as insidious as our attachment to delusion. It is best to heed the Zen adage: "Today's enlightenment is tomorrow's mistake."

Dōgen's teaching of practice/realization is his attempt to clear away notions that gradual practice will eventually result in breakthrough. He asserts that from the beginning, practice and realization relate as innate foci, without a causal connection. Practice/Realization can be said to consist of tranquility and insight. Tranquility grows out of the continuity of awareness. Insight occurs spontaneously and suddenly within the sphere of tranquility.

There is an analogy in science that describes the atemporal and acausal nature of Dōgen's practice/realization. The physics of quantum mechanics has noted when an electron orbiting in an atom has absorbed sufficient energy that would allow it to occupy a higher energy orbit, it "jumps" from the lower to the higher orbit without traveling between them. One moment the electron is "here," and in the next it is "there." A full grasp of "jumping" orbits requires an understanding beyond the usual concepts of cause and effect, inviting us to "see" in a new way. In Breakthrough, an analogous "spiritual jumping" occurs, where the fundamental misperception of an individual's sense of separateness collapses. As a result of this opening into a "new way of seeing," the dualism of practice and realization as distinct and serially connected, can no longer be supported. As with all other dualistic concepts, the practitioner now experiences them as an intimate relationship with the same atemporal and acausal nature as the orbit-jumping electrons.

The Dynamic Nature of the Natural Koan

The Natural Koan finds expression in the numerous elements portrayed on the Natural Koan Symbol, encompassing all aspects of the awakening process. It is the main feature and distinctive characteristic of each practitioner's spiritual life. The particular issues that are generated by the Natural Koan must be dealt with through conscious intent. Conscious engagement with the Natural Koan opens the practitioner to the Universal aspect of being, nurtures the growth of the Universal until awakening, and then facilitates mutual cultivation of it with the Personal aspect of being. In this process, one finds liberation from the fixed and permanent self of accumulated conditioned states and their habitual manifestations. In doing so, the practitioner reshapes the human personality as fluid and adaptive, and capable of penetrating the apparent Universal/Personal paradox.

The process of awakening illustrated by the Natural Koan Symbol contains both the traditional elements of Zen practice and the introspective method of the Resolution Sequence. While Zazen practice provides the power to uncover the composition of the self, the Resolution Sequence advances understanding of that knowledge. During Deconstruction one systematically acknowledges and clarifies the barriers to Transformation. In the integration process of Reconstruction, the intimate relationship of the interplay of dualistic pairs reaches its culmination.

Chapter 5
Employing the Resolution Sequence

The previous chapters have been devoted to offering explanations of Nonduality and the introspective method of the Resolution Sequence, as well as illustrating how this sequence can be employed as an aid for awakening when combined with Zazen. They also highlight the sequential formatting of the symbols as a way of explaining the expanding process.

This chapter will present narratives showing how three individuals made use of the method. As you will see, the process can be employed across an array of circumstances, from working with a particularly stressful and seemingly isolated situation, to a complex, multifaceted, and persistent conditioned state.

Many times, when we try to extricate ourselves from difficult life circumstances, there is a feeling of being stuck in place. This may owe to actual external constraints, or to our internal orientation toward a given situation. Most often, it is a complex web of circumstances combined with a conditioned state that forms a tight weave that holds us inflexibly bound. If you were given a rope with multiple knots to untangle, how would you go about it? Usually, we just pick a knobby spot and jiggle it until it loosens a bit, then with persistence to the task, little by little the knot comes undone. When our life becomes a tight weave, we need to jiggle it as well. How do we jiggle our life? We must pick something to work on through our directed intention and refined attention. Our issues have already presented us with the "problem" to work on.

After forty years of Zen meditation and twenty years of working with the Resolution Sequence, we have found that there is an autonomous nature to the healing process; it is revealed through the factors of our limitations. We generally know what we feel unable to do. Through awareness of what blocks our freedom, the path is laid out. It takes just a short period of time working with the method to begin to trust in our inherent wisdom and the process.

Situational Use of the Resolution Sequence

In the first example, the problem is between two coworkers. "Jenny" and "Alex" were at odds about how to proceed with a difficult business project. Their positions within the company were of equal authority, allowing neither of them to pull rank as a way of overriding the conflict. Their disagreement continued over an extended period of time, and developed into serious discord. No amount of discussion or mediation by superiors, or by peers, helped to improve the situation.

Each individual developed a grudge against the other, and each either expressed negative feelings or held them close to the surface. Yet the project required them to have frequent contact. This situation went on for several weeks without improvement, creating a great deal of stress for Jenny. It also was affecting the mood of other coworkers. Without some creative action, things would remain the same or worsen. Jenny feared she might even lose her job, and that felt intolerable to her.

For her part, Jenny recognized that the problem was severe enough to need concerted effort to change the situation. Although she was resolved to do something to improve the work environment, she nevertheless felt Alex was the source of the problem. Thus she would externalize the blame: "He makes me so angry." Identification occurred through Jenny's recognition of the seriousness of the circumstance, and her willingness to try and heal the rift.

Slowly, with the help of her Zazen practice, Jenny stopped blaming the whole situation on Alex. Through nonjudgmental reflection on the problem, she began to observe how carrying a grudge was operating within herself. By recognizing how she contributed to the discord, she was able to take responsibility for her own mental vexations. No longer blaming Alex for all her angry feelings, enabled Jenny the ability to say, "I'm so angry." In this way, Jenny achieved a Separation from the problem with Alex, and met the requirements for Awakening "a."

The observational perspective that accompanies Awakening "a" allowed Jenny a different relationship to the problem. This change continued to grow as she worked with the Development stage of Deconstruction. Information Jenny gathered through Development increased her understanding of the grudge dynamics.

She began to view and work with the afflictive emotions in her relationship with Alex as a Natural Koan. She made a thorough investigation of it by asking the questions, "*What is this grudge really about*? *What do I need to learn from it*?" Jenny intentionally put these two questions at the center of her meditation. Her initial inquiry led to the freedom to make other queries, and things began to really move when she asked herself, "*How do I know I have this grudge*?" In other words, what does this grudge feel like? What is it I'm experiencing that I call a grudge?

Jenny's first response was to become aware of a discomforting feeling in her lower abdomen. She carefully observed that vague discomfort and continued to question it. First, she focused on the location and nature of it, and found it to be a burning sensation in her lower abdomen on the right side. Then she asked, *And it burns like what*? In response, the image of a burning coal arose. Not surprisingly, it was at the exact place she'd been experiencing stomach pains, especially when she was at work. Jenny began to experiment with this information. She would cultivate the negative thoughts she had toward Alex and pay close attention to the burning sensation in her abdomen. With each negative thought a coal was added until at last there was a flaming bed of hot coals. Her investigation clearly revealed the connection between her habitual negative thinking patterns and the emotional and physical discomfort she experienced.

She now recognized the nature of the relationship between her thinking and the burning coals, and was able to understand what it is about Alex that triggered her automatic response. Working with all aspects of her grudge in this way enabled Jenny to maintain her equilibrium when she needed to deal directly with Alex. All the triggers were still in place but she began to respond differently. This took a great deal of courage and energy. The benefits of working through Separation and Development allowed Jenny to experience her discomfort with the problem as "anger arises." With that shift, she accepted full responsibility for her own mental state and entered the Maturation phase of the Resolution Sequence.

In Maturation, Jenny was able to stop "leaking" negative energy. Internally, she still experienced discomfort when dealing with Alex, but she now had the maturity to respond differently. Through her meditative examination of the issue, she could locate what generated her negative emotions, and by applying her will was able to prevent their projection into the world. She was able to embrace the entire situation, the external triggers, and her internal responses most of the time, without recourse to "turning away or touching."

Jenny experienced a breakthrough and achieved liberation from her grudge one Parents' Day at work, when she observed a tender moment between Alex and his ten-year-old daughter. Seeing Alex in a capacity other than that of a "difficult co-worker," affected her deeply, even bringing her to tears. She was surprised by the intensity of her response. Sometime later, Jenny realized she no longer experienced the harshest manifestations of her negative feelings toward Alex. She experienced a psychophysical shift brought about through the Transformation of her attitude, as relief from the severe stomach problems that plagued her daily at work. She explored this in her meditation by checking on the bed of coals. One day she was startled by what she experienced. The coals were no longer internal to her but presented themselves as a bonfire on a beach. As she watched the scene the tide came in and extinguished all the remnants of the burning coals, eventually covering over the fire pit with cool wet sand.

Jenny recognized a new openness in her interactions with Alex. Although she experienced relief from the changes she observed in her response to him, some doubt remained that the reprieve could be lasting. Jenny had reached Discerning Differences. Here the practitioner knows things are different but is unable to articulate them clearly. Careful observation initiates the next stage of Reconstruction, Clarifying Details.

In Jenny's case, she engaged in a thorough analysis of the process of "grudge to liberation." She acknowledged that her consistent meditation practice, along with concerted efforts to remain aware of her own negative emotions and refrain from expressing them, fostered the environment within which Transformation occurred. Had she not been working to resolve her conflict with Alex, would she have even noticed his interaction with his daughter? Jenny could not answer that question definitively, yet she felt certain the inner work she had done was requisite for the Transformation.

Curiously, the first thing she could articulate was that even though some of her old responses to Alex still arose on occasion, they felt "rootless," in the sense that she remained free from her old reactions to them. They were no longer the emotional traps they had been. They passed quickly and eventually subsided altogether. Jenny remained very alert in her interactions with Alex, enjoying the changes she experienced and taking special note of them. For example, she found during meetings that she remained more open to his ideas, instead of automatically becoming internally critical of them.

Within a couple of months, Jenny began to accept that her relationship to Alex was indeed changed, as least from her side. She noticed how Alex responded to other coworkers, and recognized that what had irritated her was the way he seemed to relate to everyone, not just her. She also began to understand that his aggressive attitude was an attempt to overcome his own insecurity. Each observation and realization brought Jenny more freedom. She was pleasantly surprised when she noticed that this newfound freedom extended beyond her relationship with Alex.

Jenny found that the change she effected in her relationship with Alex had an impact in other relationships, leaving her more confident to try new things in her life. She was more comfortable with herself in social situations, having gained confidence that she could deal with a really difficult situation constructively. Relief and Comfort manifested as a change in her general disposition toward her life.

The reward for her efforts was Acceptance that the changes she worked toward were enduring, which enhanced a sense of Naturalness in dealing with her life. She no longer needed to expend heroic efforts monitoring her reactions to Alex. Although she understood that her new demeanor did not guarantee that Alex would undergo any significant change, she noted small and welcome changes in attitude on his part. While he still conveyed his impatience and antagonism toward her at times, she maintained her freedom.

Working with an Identified Conditioned State

The second narrative offers an example of how one can use the Resolution Sequence to resolve an enduring, conditioned state that limits an individual's life.

"Steve" is in his mid forties. From the perspective of an outsider, his life is relatively stable and unproblematic. Yet he experiences a pervasive dissatisfaction, bordering on depression at times, but never severe enough to requirc therapeutic intervention.

Steve has been a Zen practitioner for a little over ten years. When asked why he practices Zazen, he responds that he enjoys the companionship of like-minded people and finds Zen ritual meaningful in ways not true of other religions he has explored. He adds that he usually feels better after Zazen, and that the philosophical orientation and meditative practice help him cope.

One evening during meditation, Steve became overwhelmed by an intense sadness. He was unable to determine its cause. Yet the feeling was familiar, as if the melancholy were the continuous undertone of his life experience. It was always lurking there, though much of the time because of the hectic demands of his life, he was able to ignore it. He identified with the feeling of this sadness, and thought to himself, *That's just the way I am.* Still, he realized with some chagrin, that he could not remember the last time he was free of it. This sadness, to some degree, was always present.

Despite the fact that he told himself, *that's just the way I am*, he longed to be different in a way he could not articulate. Before the meditation ended he committed to understanding what lay behind his propensity toward sadness.

At this point, Steve has become aware of the conditioned state of sadness in a new way. Identification, the first step of the Resolution Sequence, has taken place. Over a period of weeks and months Steve makes great effort to become aware of the nuances of his sadness, what precipitates its varying intensity, and the duration of the severe episodes. Now, his conscious efforts have rewarded him with memories, and he is able to recognize what triggers them. All this has helped him clarify and articulate the problem.

One evening during Zazen, he gained an important insight. He understood that he experienced a milieu of reticence towards his life, and that this reticence was the source of his sadness.

The issue was no longer, "that's just the way I am." Reticence was something he could deal with from a different perspective. There was a new relationship to the problem that came through Separation, one that invigorated Steve's inquiry and desire for change. At this point Steve has experienced Awakening "a." Just as successful Identification initiates Separation, Separation encourages Development. Steve now could experience compassion for himself, and acknowledge the efforts he has made to cope with the issue.

Now Steve was able to see that the issue of his reticence has prevented him from doing and becoming all that he might be capable of. This led to his understanding that reticence was the origin of his dissatisfaction and sadness. His Zazen practice provided key support for all Steve's efforts. He continued to explore all sides of the issue with a compassionate inquiry, combined with nonjudgmental awareness of the truth of his life circumstances. The more open he became, the more information he received.

Working on Development naturally leads to Maturation. He experienced satisfaction from having worked constructively with the problem of reticence, but was still aware of its continuing presence in his life. The sadness, too, had lessened but he knew he was not free from its influence. Steve continued to make small conscious changes that benefited his life, but some discomfort caused by the habit of reticence continued. It was something that he always needed to consciously override.

With Maturation, we have come to the critical juncture of Deconstruction. The stages of Deconstruction comprise the cognitive understanding of the inhibiting dynamic gained through Zazen – Introspection. Maturation is as far as one can go with a conditioned state prior to Transformation. This phase may go on indefinitely or throughout the remainder of an individual's life, and it is all one can do until Transformation occurs. A transformative experience is required to take resolution further. Transformative experiences occur in two forms, in an infinite variety of ways.

In the first form, a transformative experience is linked to a seemingly innocuous event. A ready example is Buddha looking up and seeing the morning star, or Jenny observing Alex interact with his daughter. The second form arises through liberating insight cultivated through effort in Zazen. For Steve it occurred in the following way.

One night during evening Zazen, Steve experienced a liberating insight. He was not concentrating on reticence at the time, and hadn't done so in quite a while. In fact, he was enjoying a rare moment of peace with himself and the world.

What suddenly revealed itself to him transformed his relationship to the problem of reticence. Steve experienced an intuitive vision of his mother, maternal grandfather, and ancestors he didn't know, forming a line of individuals without end. Altogether, his ancestors bowed to him in the formal Zen manner of greeting and respect. Within that moment he intuitively *knew* that each of them had also struggled with the issue of reticence. He had no doubt that was the meaning of the image. It only lasted seconds, but it was transformative.

Through that brief vision Steve was relieved of a sense of shame he had not consciously experienced before. The shame lay secretly imbedded within his conditioned state of reticence, outside of his awareness. Until that insight, he was unaware of the degree of shame he had always carried. Shame was the result of not wholeheartedly living his life, the legacy of reticence. He also recognized that it was not just his personal problem—proof that there was something inherently wrong with him. Rather, he saw it was an inherited trait that had been passed down the maternal line of his family for generations.

Relief from a sense of personal shame was extremely freeing for him. It was the missing element that completed resolution of the dynamics associated with reticence. Steve could now stand in the correct relationship to that particular conditioned state. There was no longer need for shame. There was only the need to be responsible and to work on the dynamics of reticence. He fulfilled that responsibility through his work with the Deconstruction side of the Resolution Sequence. It was as if his whole ancestral family had blessed his efforts.

At the time of the insight, Steve also experienced a Psychophysical Shift. This manifested as an opening in the *hara* [22] that welcomed the breath deeper than he had experienced before. Tears of joy and gratitude accompanied all this. Steve had experienced Awakening "A," a change of being that would soon result in significant changes in behavior.

Transformation now brought Steve to the Reconstruction side of the Resolution Sequence. One might ask, "If Transformation has occurred, is it really necessary to actively engage in Reconstruction?" "Will the benefits of the Transformation elapse if it is not undertaken?" The benefit of working with Reconstruction is that it continues the awakening process. Without it, one's changes have a tendency to remain naive. The more conscious we become, the more we can appreciate the rewards of working toward awakening. As we gain experience with the complete Resolution Sequence, we can work through subsequent conditioned states with greater ease, in less time. This is possible because our trust and confidence in ourselves, and the process have increased. This trust and confidence is the outcome of articulating the change of being through the observation of new behaviors enhanced through working with the stages of Reconstruction.

From the moment Steve experienced the Psychophysical Shift of his breath, he felt a continued freedom with it. He felt lighter throughout his body. There was a brief period of disorientation that lasted a few days, brought on by the newness of what he was feeling. It was so different, although very pleasant. He just didn't know what to make of it all. And yet, what he was experiencing was exactly how he always knew he should feel. It was startling. This type of experience defines Discerning Differences.

Clarifying Details came next in the process. After a few days of enjoying the overall difference in feeling toward his life, Steve gained the ability to articulate clearly the changes he was experiencing. Steve became aware of feeling that his physical movements were more fluid. Before, he felt as if there was a physical barrier "like a plexiglas shield" between himself and the world. Since he could see through it but not penetrate it, he never felt himself to be truly "present" in any circumstance. Now he experienced "being there." Steve also noticed that could he voice his opinion at work without hesitation, and no longer felt exposed after having done so. That was a huge change. At the same time, his relationship with his family improved. He was more skillful in loving and caring of his wife and children, and felt worthy of their affection. Most startling to Steve was the fact that he signed up for art classes about six months later. That was something he'd always wanted to do.

Clarification can go on indefinitely, as one encounters life situations with increased openness and new ways of responding. The changes that come with it can be quite subtle.

Acceptance is the stage of Reconstruction where the individual believes a new change can be enduring. Although at first Steve was delighted with the changes he was experiencing, he doubted that they would prove long-lasting. This is common during the first stages of Reconstruction. Only time and close observation will bring a practitioner to Acceptance. While each individual has a unique threshold for Acceptance, it usually requires only a month or so to acknowledge, "I'm really different."

Once Acceptance occurs, Relief and Comfort arrive swiftly: one simply lives the changes. Naturalness is the result of working with Reconstruction. People often express difficulty remembering how they were before the resolution of their problem. It is lovely to witness an individual become free to be the person he/she always wanted to be.

In the first narrative, Jenny's story is evoked in a way that resembles how we tend to experience our problems, that is, immersed in the turmoil. After her issue was resolved, Jenny was more clearly able to reflect on and discern the stages by which this was achieved. The resolution of conditioned states is more or less subject to this process, whether or not an individual is conscious of it. It is common for a beginner using the Resolution Sequence to understand its dynamics only in retrospect, when the process is complete. By contrast, Steve's story indicates a more conscious use.

It is quite empowering to understand the nature of the Resolution Sequence and have the ability to encounter problems with confidence, rather than feel incapacitated in the face of them. The following narrative, Robert's story, reflects many years of an individual's work with a life-long problem.

The Pervasive Influence of a Conditioned State

When Robert reflects on his relationship to what he refers to as "my problem with authority," he sees its origin at the earliest stages of his life. His father died when he was seven, leaving his mother overwhelmed with the care of her five children under age ten. He found very little direction in the home environment since his mother was kept busy just providing food for the table and buying shoes. With great admiration for her, Robert notes, "We never missed a meal."

To complicate matters, as one of the two oldest of his siblings, he was burdened with premature expectations of responsibility. By age eight, he frequently found himself in a position of authority, needing to care for his younger brothers, without a model or enough life experience for fulfilling the role of a caretaker.

One day, when he was only nine years old and babysitting, his two-year-old brother went into convulsions. There was no 911 emergency number to call at that time. He did the best he could, but the traces of that experience did not evaporate when the event was over. The biggest problems arise with difficult, negative, or traumatic experiences, as they initiate conditioned states.

Later in his work life, Robert would find himself repeatedly placed in positions of responsibility without the commensurate authority to fully perform his duties. This would be a source of great stress for him throughout his career. The hierarchical structure within the organizations that employed him ensured that his frustration would be ongoing. More will be said about such replicating patterns later. For now, they serve to underscore the enduring influence of our earliest experiences, which remain at the root of our karmic patterns. These patterns, in turn, replicate themselves over and over until we apply our intention and attention to resolve them. This karmic outcome does not happen because we are bad or evil or deserve punishment. It is just the form our human life takes.

Robert's work life proved a "variation on a theme"— too much responsibility, too little authority to fulfill it. Although his relationship with authority differed from when he was a child, the degree of anxiety, stress, and discomfort in his work environment left him essentially in the same emotional state. The story of how this theme played out is intricately connected to the whole of his life, and to all of the work he has done to resolve his entanglement with it.

By the time Robert was twenty-one years old, he was living quite an alienated and unhappy life. He briefly met with some success during his tour of duty in the Navy, gaining confidence in his technical ability when he trained as an electronics technician. The military also served to widen his view of life by exposing him to a great number of young men from diverse backgrounds, as well as the opportunity to travel abroad. Along with these benefits, the nature of the institution—wherein roles are very prescribed—made it a safe container and offered a reprieve from his "authority issue." However, the well-oiled machine of military order did not provide enough comfort for him to consider becoming a "lifer."

Once discharged from the Navy, Robert's Natural Koan with authority was energized, and impacted almost all of his relationships. On the job, interaction with supervisors was stressful. Associations with co-workers and personal friendships were poor and unsatisfying. He had difficulty in establishing intimate relationships. Robert describes the emotional tenor of his life at this time as being "angry and defensive."

One's Natural Koan contains an intriguing irony. From the inside, it feels unsolvable, yet one cannot stop trying to do so, unless we resort to the soul killing activities of alcohol, drugs, excessive sensuality, becoming a workaholic, and a host of other behaviors our culture offers for the general purpose of deadening our life. We might try to solve our existential pain by losing ourselves in these behaviors while we are young, because we do not know what else to do. Eventually we may recognize these behaviors do not lead anywhere we really want to go.

Luckily for Robert, he began a search for what might lie beyond the scope of cultural sedation. He moved to San Francisco in 1965, and by serendipitous good fortune stumbled into the Metaphysical Library. Now, there was a world he could get into! Well-intentioned librarians supported his initiation into this new world with recommendations for book after book, which he devoured. Part of this exploration included coming into contact with Buddhism through Theravadin texts. These, however, he found "unemotional, analytic, and scholastic." He was not inclined to pursue Buddhism at this point, although he regarded "the Buddha's fundamental teaching of life's problems in the Four Noble Truths as a clear and logical expression of the human condition."

Robert spent three years in pursuit of a resonant worldview before another fortuitous incident brought him in contact with Zen. At the age of twenty-five he decided to move from San Francisco to a city in the Midwest, where one of his younger brothers was living. The night before leaving town he attended a party. There he had a one-time encounter with an individual who gave him a book to read on the train east. The book was *Zen in the Art of Archery* by Eugen Herrigel, and it was to have a profound impact on Robert. It was after reading that book, which described the awakening of a Westerner, that the full import of the Buddha's teaching grew beyond a casual interest into a lifelong pursuit.

What happened next sounds like a contrived movie script. Only four days after arriving in town, Robert was riding a bus to a store in pursuit of a black Stetson hat. At one of the bus stops he looked up and saw a sign for a local Zen Center. He immediately got off the bus and soon met up with his first Zen teacher. He never did get the hat. For Robert, just reading the book had been a visceral experience that quelled his doubts about what he should be doing. It revealed a whole new vision of the world. The possibility of awakening offered him the meaningful relationship to his life that he was searching for. Three years passed between finding the Metaphysical Library and reading *Zen in the Art of Archery*. The synchronicity of encountering a Zen center so soon after finishing the book still amazes him.

Robert spent a brief time with this first teacher before deciding to return to San Francisco to attend the Zen Center there. Although he was unfamiliar with the Resolution Sequence at this time in his life, upon reflection, he recognizes that he had entered the Separation phase. He now understands that the observational viewpoint and questioning attitude gained through Zazen allowed him to identify and work directly with his authority koan. After only a year in San Francisco, Robert moved to Southern California to study with the first Zen priest he met, who had recently relocated there, and assisted in the development of a new Zen Center. There was a more personal connection with this teacher than the previous center afforded him.

Robert acknowledges that, while his painful existential state was mitigated somewhat by his confidence in the Buddha's teaching and commitment to Zazen practice, his relationships were only marginally better. Recognition of his primary conditioned states of insecurity, anger, and defensiveness became more apparent during his first two years of practice at the new center. In addition, his authority issues were exacerbated by intimate contact with a Zen teacher. Though difficult, this experience would ultimately prove to be a good thing. The relationship with a Zen teacher often proves problematic for beginners, and not at all what we imagined it would be.

As a result of Robert's difficulty with his teacher, he progressed to the Development phase of the Resolution Sequence. Precisely because the relationship was nothing like he imagined, he was forced to investigate the intensely painful reactions he experienced to the authority of his teacher. It is not uncommon for young and naïve individuals struggling to gain a sense of autonomy to idealize significant others in their lives, especially authority figures, and to endow them with attributes that they may, or may not, possess. When we idealize another, like a Zen teacher, we assign to that individual the qualities we long to embody. In a healthy relationship, the "idealized" individual understands the nature of this transference and holds it in trust, until the student develops said traits and can retract the projection. At that time the teacher/student relationship becomes more equal and collegial.

Before that time, however, when the idealized individual behaves in ways that are troubling or disappointing, it causes confusion in the student that can be quite devastating. This is bound to happen because no one, except possibly a Buddha, can fulfill such idealized expectations. The clay feet must be exposed.

If they are not, the student may remain in a naïve relationship to the teacher to the detriment of his own development.

Complicating Robert's relationship with this teacher was the mix of their personalities, and the cultural clash of a middle aged Japanese Zen priest attempting to train a young American in the late 1960s and early 1970s.

Nevertheless, within four years, the work with his authority issue brought Robert to the Maturation stage of the Resolution Sequence. By this time, he clearly saw which part of the problem was his responsibility, and which part his teacher contributed. He could now deal with his teacher's eccentricities without expressing anger or defensiveness, although he still experienced those emotions in dealing with him.

Robert began thinking about leaving California, a decision complicated by the extent of involvement with the Zen Center, and the responsibility he felt toward it. When a person can see a difficult situation clearly, but is unable to act on a solution, it can generate just the right creative tension to bring forth Transformation.

One evening while Robert sat alone in the zendo, just such a transformative moment happened. Because of his history, up until this point he had a poor sense of self and thus a weak sense of his own authority in relationship to others. He would attempt to determine what he needed to do in his own life, based on what he thought others in his situation might do. On this particular evening, this whole dynamic collapsed in the wake of Robert's transformative insight that, *My life is my teacher*. It was the answer to his koan. With it came a nascent understanding into the nature of spiritual autonomy, the heart of authentic authority. He saw that authenticity cannot be achieved by association. Completely integrating his understanding, however, would take many years. The Psychophysical Shift that accompanied this breakthrough was neither pleasant, nor a relief. Robert recognized that he was completely exhausted from years of striving to please, and from working too hard.

Robert worked to extricate himself from his circumstance and was able to leave a year later. Had he seen any other alternative, he may not have stayed that long. He now recognizes that the time he remained at the Center after his transformative insight served to reinforce the change. From an outside perspective, things might have appeared unchanged; from within, Robert understood that everything had changed.

Once he left, it took several years to regain his health. Understanding that his life was his teacher brought a tremendous shift in Robert's orientation to others in positions of authority. He no longer assumed that just because someone held a position, it meant that the individual was either competent or well-intentioned. He was no longer malleable in naïve ways, giving authority over himself to another.

After leaving the Center, Robert relocated to another part of the country. He continued Zen practice with a different teacher, establishing a healthier relationship that reflected who he had become. The long process of integration continued. For Robert, Awakening "a" brought awareness of, and responsibility for, the problems he had in all his relationships. There is a significant shift when an individual stops blaming external sources for their unhappiness, and one begins to ask, "What can I do differently?" The work of Identification, Separation, and Development is continually defining for oneself the nature of the problem and its history.

It is worth noting that the Reconstruction side of the Resolution Sequence is not painful in the way Deconstruction is, but it does require continuous observation. The habit energies of an entrenched conditioned state do not dissolve at Transformation. Reconstruction is working with their dynamic energy to their complete resolution. Sometimes this work can go on for years. The length of time that this takes depends on the strength of the original conditioned state. Many are complex, multifaceted, and form a thick thread that binds us to the tight weave of our karmic pattern, affecting almost every aspect of our life.

Robert worked on Discerning Differences and Clarifying Details through Acceptance in subsequent years. After he relocated, most of his relationships improved. He married, raised a family, and was successful in building a career in business. He made and maintained many meaningful friendships. His sense of inner authority increased as he matured and allowed for a healthy "sense of self." The one problematic area that persisted was in his relationships with managers at work who oversaw his position. There was still a tiny hook that forestalled complete resolution of the authority issue.

Robert hovered for a long time at the Acceptance phase of the Resolution Sequence. It took years for Relief and Comfort to bring forth Naturalness in his work environment. Perhaps if he had chosen a different career path the timing might have been different, though it is likely the hook would probably still have been in play. Spiritual competence requires developmental progress for one's emotional and psychological growth. It cannot replace life experience. There was one more step before achieving complete relief from the authority koan. That step was intimately related to his professional life as a manager.

Serious problems in the work environment were his responsibility, but he was generally hampered from resolving them to his satisfaction by upper management, who put arbitrary conditions on how things must be done. Some circumstances even included significant safety issues for other employees, for which he felt great concern. The limitations imposed by higher management precluded Robert from solving problems in the way he felt was best. This challenge to his authentic authority was the source of continued stress.

It was fifteen years into his work career before Robert came into contact with the Resolution Sequence. He employed it many times when encountering difficulties with corporate executives who oversaw his department. The Resolution Sequence helped him maintain the proper orientation toward his difficulties at work. He was able to manage his emotional tenor with, sometimes, abusive supervision. He was able to sustain his own self-worth in the face of opposing opinions.

As is wont to happen, the moment of complete freedom arrived unexpectedly, during a typical business meeting. Robert was presenting information to the executive planning committee of his company. These meetings were oftentimes contentious, and he repeatedly felt stressed having to defend what he was doing. At this particular meeting, he was free of an internally defensive stance, and had his presentation well prepared. No sooner had he begun than one Vice President interrupted him, as usual, with a somewhat accusatory question. Instead of stopping what he was saying and deferring to this rude interruption, Robert suggested in a completely guileless manner, "Let's just hold that a moment," and completed his presentation. He had never experienced anything quite like the freedom of that moment. It did not go unnoticed by other participants, either. Three other executives came up to him after the meeting, and each essentially asked, "What happened in there?" For the first time, others witnessed the unseemly behavior of Robert's longtime nemesis, which he found somewhat satisfying.

At the moment of his response, Robert was released from the last hook of the authority koan and experienced Awakening "AA." In the weeks following the meeting, his sense of Naturalness in the work environment continued. Robert had gained Awakening "A" with "my life is my teacher." The "hook" was Robert's desire to be recognized by people in authority as being competent. There is nothing wrong with wanting recognition for a job well done. It seems a natural wish of a hard working individual. Needing it is what sets the hook. When he let go of needing that recognition, he was no longer hooked to the last remnants of the myriad habit energies of the authority koan. He gained real freedom. Truly letting go of needing any confirmation from an outside source completed his sense of autonomy. That degree of letting go cannot be willed, and we cannot feign the truth.

Robert continued to enjoy that freedom and sense of Naturalness at work until his retirement.

Now the question is, why have we told this narrative, and how is this story a good example of the awakening process? The answer lies in the phrase "awakening *process*," with the emphasis on process. We offer it exactly because it portrays so well the level of work many conditioned states require for resolution. They can be tenacious in the influence they exert on an individual's life.

The Buddha practiced many spiritual disciplines for six years before sitting alone beneath the Bodhi tree, vowing not to rise until he resolved the question, "Why is there suffering in the world?" The wonderful stories we read about a Zen master's awakening intrigue us, but they do not convey the excruciating history of that individual's existential dilemma. The transformative moments, like all other phenomena in this world, result from concatenation of causes and conditions. One important aspect of those conditions is the conscious effort of the individual to awaken.

We may need to free ourselves of afflictive emotions in what seem like isolated circumstances. We may need to work on a limiting trait that keeps us cloistered and prevents us from living freely in the world. We may also need to work a lifetime to cut the threads of the tight weave of our karma before the design of our life can begin to take on a new pattern. And really, we need to do all of this at the same time.

Katagiri Roshi used to say that when a mother bird sensed that her baby bird was about to hatch and starting pecking from the inside, she would peck from the outside. When we work consciously to awaken, through our efforts in meditation and other skillful means such as the Resolution Sequence, this is how we peck from the inside. Moments of Transformation can be likened to the mother bird pecking from the outside. They are the gifts that complete the cracking open of the hard shell of condition states, and we emerge into a new state of being.

Chapter 6
SHIKANTAZA

Shikantaza, Zazen only, and "just sitting" are interchangeable terms that denote a particular meditative practice. The mature form of *shikantaza* is one of spiritual power, independence, and freedom. One's emotions and intellect become refined and sensitive, open to the appreciation of human endeavor and the beauty of nature. Mastery of Zazen – Introspection frees the practitioner from the tyranny of conditioned states, and engenders the ever-creative movement of the Naturalness that arises with Awakening "AA."

Only the wholeness of the ellipse and the dynamic movement of the triangle and arrowheads remain on Figure 5, the *Shikantaza* Symbol, shown on the following page. The descriptors of the Nonduality – Resolution Sequence Symbol are no longer depicted. Instead of the textual and geometric references, the answer lies in the concordant interplay between the foci of practice/realization. This is authentic Zen practice. The harmony that "suddenly" arises in Awakening "A" is perfected in Awakening "AA." Even though the *Shikantaza* Symbol appears simple and

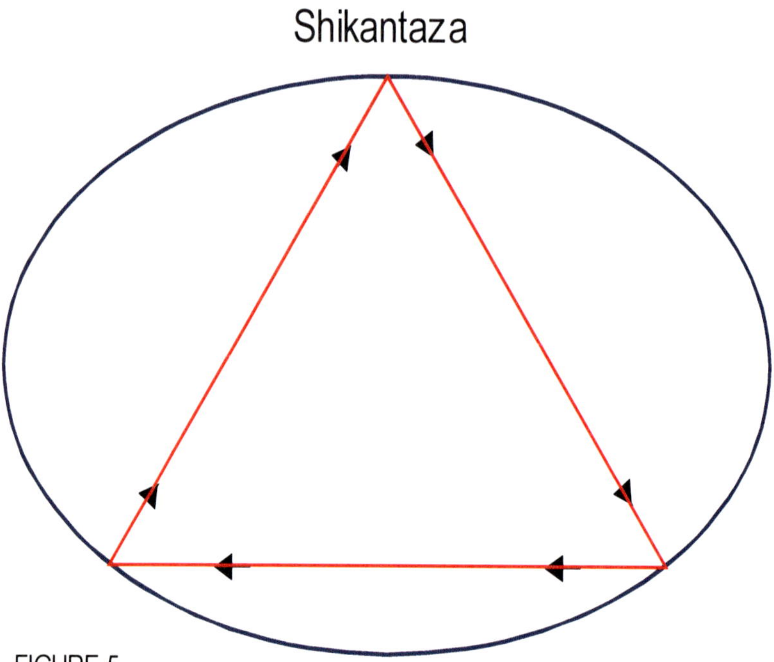

FIGURE 5

shorn of any expansive meaning, the remaining elements express an in-depth experience.

One who wishes to master Zazen – Introspection must be prepared to make innumerable trips around the triangle to resolve the mountain of conditioned states. For this reason, the triangle and the arrowheads of the *Shikantaza* Symbol paint a picture of continuous complementary movement of dualities; and the ellipse encompasses their movement. Together, the triangle and ellipse illustrate the unitary relationship of Dōgen's practice/realization.

The modern conception of "mind" as a psychological and mental entity fails to convey the mind transmitted by Buddhas and

Ancestors. The mind of *shikantaza* validates that all phenomena express universal truth, that mind extends throughout all phenomena, and that all phenomena are inseparable from mind. The indivisible nature of reality goes far beyond the implications of psychology. Our initial perception of the natural world is misleading as to the true nature of reality. In practice we refine our sense of the world with observation and inquiry. The effort yields a picture of the world completely different from the one we confront in our everyday experience. The solidity of "things" and "objects," mental or physical, inner or outer, dissolves in the face of the Buddhist teaching of Emptiness.

The following descriptions of four attributes of *shikantaza* allude to the effects its practice has on an individual.

Dynamic Movement

In *shikantaza*, both the inner and outer worlds change rapidly. We discover our thoughts and moods to be especially labile. Activities that we formerly took to be enduring, we now know to be transient, without lasting substance. They exist in ever-changing forms rooted in causes and conditions, and all eventually pass away. Trust in the process results in our unconstrained dynamic movement around the triangle. *Shikantaza*, as shown on the symbol, exemplifies Emptiness, the teaching that sets Buddhism apart from other religions.

The basic instruction in *shikantaza* is to sit attentively and observe the process and contents of the mind and body. *Shikantaza* rests on nonjudgmental awareness within actual Zazen practice. However, it must be noted that viewing nonjudgmently does not mean we turn a blind eye toward the intuitive information that arises within practice. The proper attitude toward thought is one of nonpreferential discernment.

Inclusiveness

An example of inclusiveness is demonstrated in the following story of a newly ordained monk. Upon receiving his *o-kesa* [a monk's robe] his teacher instructed him to care for it as if it were his eyes. The monk followed this instruction, insuring that the robe was kept clean and repaired as necessary. In time, his concerned attention spread from his o-kesa to other objects he encountered in his life, and eventually the barrier that creates a false sense of separation eroded. He understood that all beings deserve the same respect because all arise from the same *Buddhanature.*

The equality and interdependence one finds in *shikantaza* replaces the misunderstanding of separateness. *Shikantaza* discloses the vision of the unity of all phenomena; one recognizes *Buddhanature*, the clarity that issues forth from its embodiment, is recognized to be the very core of every being.

Awakening

In *shikantaza*, the practitioner achieves mastery of the relationship of thinking and not-thinking. Hee-Jin Kim describes the successful outcome this way: "Thus in his [Dōgen's] Zen, both experience and thought are at once deconstructed and reconstructed through non-thinking; they are therefore free from bifurcation without compromising their differences and tensions."[23] Conscious participation in the movements of Deconstruction and Reconstruction around the triangle creates the transformative power of awakening. Perspectives change, and being and behavior transform.

Dōgen echoes the ancient teaching of the founders of Zen when using the terms thinking, not-thinking, and nonthinking. He might have used feeling, not-feeling, and nonfeeling, thus centering Nonduality on emotions rather than thought. The same could be said for will, not-will, and nonwill, putting the emphasis on volition. This tripartite approach remains valid for other manifestations as well, such as form or perception. One's observation and inquiry provide the key means [not-xxxxing] for achieving accurate insight into one's emotional and willful processes and their content. In *shikantaza*, direct experience replaces explanations and retrospection.

Intimacy

Shikantaza is regarded by many to be the highest form of meditative practice. Practitioners commit themselves to sharing the fruits of awakening. *Shikantaza* perfects the Zen practice of heart-to-heart communication. The process of Deconstruction gives birth to a nascent compassion; in Reconstruction, our newfound compassion matures and finds completion in service to others.

Hee-Jin Kim explains: "For Dōgen's part, his Zen shifts attention from the simple interior state of mind to all the realities of the universe.... In other words, meditation is not so much a retreat from the external world as it is an opening of the body-mind to the mystery of the inner and outer world and beyond."[24] It is the actualization of the Middle Way of Mahayana Buddhism.

Intimacy is where individual and social responsibilities are of equal significance, as revealed in this story from the Record of Tung-shan.

> When Tung-shan was about to take his leave, Nan-yuan said, "Make a thorough study of the BuddhaDharma, and broadly benefit the world."
>
> Tung-shan inquired, "I have no question about studying the BuddhaDharma, but what is it to broadly benefit the world?"
>
> Nan-yuan replied, "Not to disregard a single being."[25]

Nan-yuan clarifies the definition and field of social ethics generated in the mind of the *shikantaza* practitioner. "Not to disregard a single being" recognizes the equality of every form of life without exception, and brings that wisdom to bear in daily encounters. Practitioners learn that the ordinary events of life are the cultivation of practice and the way of Transformation.

Zen is unremitting practice—perpetual awakening. Perpetual awakening deepens the well of wisdom and unveils previously unseen paths to compassionate action. "Taking one step forward, buddhas and ancestors come. Taking one step backward, expose every bit of your heart."[26] Dōgen's thirteenth-century assertion offers a foundation for twenty-first century Zen social ethics. As members in the community of Dharma-beings, we find ourselves living within a non-negotiable web of intricate relations. Committing ourselves to the Deconstruction of conditioned states opens the mind to the vastness of being. Advancing through the stages of Reconstruction offers its benefits to the world without equivocation.

Last Thoughts

After returning from China, Dōgen wrote the *Fukanzazengi* [Universal Instructions for the Practice of Zazen], wherein he wrote, "You have gained the pivotal opportunity of human form."[27] Our human form—physical and mental—provides an amazing instrument, one capable of recognizing the value of awakening, as well as being able to consciously work to embody its profound effects.

Dōgen goes on to say, "You are maintaining the essential working of the Buddha Way."[28] What is the Buddha Way, and how is it maintained? The answer to both parts of the question is the same—the process of awakening itself. Awakening lies at the heart of resolving the fundamental misperception and attaining the mind of freedom, naturalness, and service. Sometime in the distant past, an ancestor of ours discovered awakening. Buddha claimed he rediscovered it. As disciples of Buddha, we tread the path with other "children of fire," together honoring our undeniable aspiration to awaken.

APPENDIX
INTRODUCTION TO METAPHOR AWARENESS

The content of this book presents a skillful means for dealing with conditioned states through learning and using the Resolution Sequence. This appendix focuses on a particular method of employing the Resolution Sequence.

After retiring as a practicing psychotherapist, I [Barbara] formulated a process that translated David Grove's Metaphor Therapy into a format more conducive to working with conditioned states as part of an individual's meditative experience. I call this method Metaphor Awareness. It is essentially Grove's original work with a few changes and one major addition. Grove's system outlined no stages for Reconstruction; Metaphor Awareness process addresses this lack.

Another significant difference compared with Grove's model concerns when and under what circumstances Metaphor Awareness is best employed. Working with metaphors as either Metaphor Therapy or Metaphor Awareness is equally beneficial.

However, as an awareness practice, it can be viewed more as an interactive meditation within the relationship of practitioner and facilitator. Metaphor Awareness is most appropriate for the practitioner who has worked the Resolution Sequence in Deconstruction, and who maintains Maturation [emotional stability] with an issue. The process can then be employed to initiate Transformation.

The practice of Zen meditation, particularly *shikantaza* of the Soto tradition, is uniquely compatible with the process of Metaphor Awareness. Skills necessary for meditation are the same as those required for Metaphor Awareness: clarity of intention and nonjudgmental attention. Zen meditation and Metaphor Awareness offer unlimited potential for beneficial change, both subtle and profound.

Metaphor Awareness is a respectful and elegant process by which we can define the form of a particular problem through a state of purposeful and focused attention. Through a precise and nonintrusive method of investigation, metaphors arise and give form and clarity to our psychic landscape.

Working metaphorically allows interaction with our internal processes in ways that just relating our experience cannot accomplish. The Metaphor Awareness process is mysterious and incomprehensible to our ordinary dualistic mindset, yet intriguing enough to engage our full and necessary cooperation. Metaphor Awareness, like Zen meditation, allows direct participation with the wisdom of the nondual mind through our active attention.

Metaphors, within the Metaphor Awareness process, are containers by which we symbolically record and store the history of negative experiences. Although metaphors are commonly used in conversation, we usually miss the information they convey. ["Sometimes my boss just burns me up."] The healing potential of a metaphor exists just beneath the surface of our ordinary consciousness and is highly charged with personal meaning. Metaphors are usually considered literary devices for evoking a comparison or poetically expressing an idea. Here they are seen as the psychophysical manifestation of an existential condition, and we can work with them accordingly.

The existence of a metaphor indicates the incomplete resolution of an experience. Originally, it arose as an attempt to protect oneself during stressful events. It becomes a problem when it continues to influence our feelings and behavior long after an experience is over. The presence of metaphors reveals the habitual responses [conditioned states] we find most disturbing and interfering to the way we would like to respond to life.

Working with a conditioned state through Metaphor Awareness relies solely on an individual's own insight, intuition, and tacit knowledge in determining how resolution should occur. The process begins by refining our intention. This is accomplished by the practitioner answering the question, "What do you want?" The goal that we formulate, and the language we choose to articulate it, allows us to locate and develop our personal metaphors. From the practitioner's own choice of words, metaphors are located and developed [Anger "like a burning torch in the throat," fear in the stomach "like a clenched iron fist," confusion behind the eyes "like a swirling dark cloud]. These metaphors contain information that goes far beyond our ordinary understanding of the words used, such as "like an iron fist" or "like an burning torch." Metaphors are the language of one's primary experience. It is the experience itself, because they contain the history of the conditioned state and hold the elements to heal it.[29]

After identifying the metaphors, the interactive process allows direct communication with the images through the facilitator's practice of "Clean Language." Clean Language is the method of inquiry developed by Dave Grove, of which Ernest Rossi said, "A gentle genie has escaped from the lamp. His name is David Grove and his magic is Clean Language."

In response to Clean Language inquiries, the information symbolically encoded within the metaphor unfolds in discrete increments. The metaphors reveal their purpose and wisdom, and then transform. Transformation of the metaphoric landscape enduringly alters our internal ecology and allows us to respond to our lives with greater freedom and spontaneity.

Figure 6 – Symbol for Metaphor Awareness

This version of the symbol introduces a few new terms: Metaphor Awareness [described above], T-1 Trapped in Time, Clean Language, and T+1 Freedom are added to the Resolution Sequence.

T-1 [Trapped in Time]

T-1 is the term for the operation of a conditioned state in Metaphor Awareness. It represents some seconds or minutes before the worst moment of an event that becomes imprinted as a conditioned state. In Metaphor Therapy, Grove developed a unique perspective of

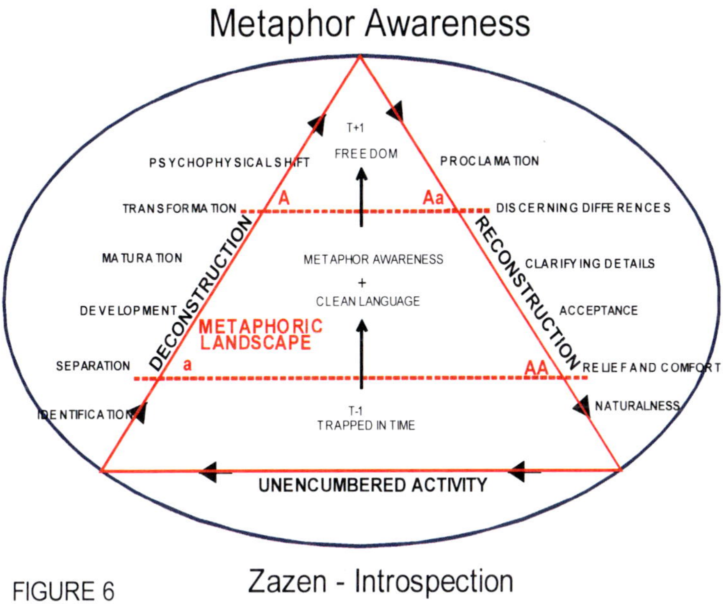

FIGURE 6

what happens when a conditioned state arises, although he never referred to the mechanics of it as a conditioned state. He saw the origin of conditioned states as the incomplete processing of negative events.

A negative event is not something we want to go through. We would prefer to stop what is happening. But to do that, we would have to freeze time. While we cannot literally freeze time and stop the event, it is as if a fragment of ourselves stops time and remains frozen some minutes or seconds before the worst moment of the experience. This fragment [Figure Within] is the dynamic that is triggered when subsequent circumstances initiate the resulting conditioned state.

The individual for whom the moment is frozen in time, his/her thoughts and feelings about what is happening, as well as the environment in which it is happening, are all stored as an undifferentiated information mass somewhere in the body. This, then, expresses as a symptom [anger in the throat, fear in the stomach, confusion behind the eyes]. The Figure Within does not complete the experience even though it has occurred. It is "trapped in time" before the worst moment of that experience. It does not age. It does not know what happens. It does not know it survived the experience. It replicates the same feelings over and over when the conditioned state is activated. The individual has little or no control over the psychophysical ramifications of its symptoms. A person experiencing the activation of an intense conditioned state feels totally overwhelmed, overtaken, and cut off from his/her usual coping mechanisms. This happens because the Figure Within "lives" there and retains custody of those feelings. The symptoms cannot be eliminated without destroying a portion of the individual.

Resolution of a conditioned state can only occur when the Figure Within is freed from the "time-trap" in which it is caught. Freeing the Figure Within is the goal of Metaphor Awareness, and it is the Figure Within that determines how resolution should occur. All the dynamics of a T-1 state occur whether or not the individual remembers the event. An example of a T-1 state would be a car accident we might have been in. Even if everyone is okay, for a while we may still relive the accident over and over. The part we relive is the moment *just before* the impact. Similarly, veterans with Posttraumatic Stress Disorder report reliving, over and over, the moment *just before* the explosion, or *just before* their buddy was killed. As noted earlier, whether or not one experiences an event as negative is entirely subjective. Thus, many experiences far less intense than a car accident or being in a war, or even seemingly benign experiences, can give rise to conditioned states.

Clean Language – Linguistic Rules for Facilitating Metaphor Sessions

Clean Language refers to precise linguistic rules that guide a Metaphor Awareness session. These rules foster the state of concentration necessary for metaphor work. It allows effective communication with nonconscious processes, avoids contamination of the practitioner's experience by the facilitator's biases or expectations, and resonates with the practitioner to assist in the transformation of words into physiological imagery. [Examples of Clean Language are provided in the Resolution Sequence of a Metaphor Awareness Session]

Rules of Clean Language

Avoid eye contact between the facilitator and practitioner.

Speak more slowly than normal, in a soft voice.

Repeat verbatim what the practitioner says.

Base each subsequent question on the last statement of the practitioner.

Match verb form and tense with practitioner's statement.

> Pose questions in the subjunctive mood. Invite elements to do things, never tell them what to do. "And would an iron fist in stomach be interested in…"
>
> Never use the definite article "the."
>
> Do not use "you," unless the practitioner uses "I."
>
> Use the pronouns "he" or "she" only if they originate from the practitioner.
>
> Begin each statement with "And."

T+1 [Freedom]

T+1 refers to the time just *after* the worst moment of an experience. All elements found in the T-1 metaphor landscape are transformed in T+1. When the metaphoric landscape transforms and releases the Figure Within, the conditioned state is resolved.

Resolution Sequence of a Metaphor Awareness Session

Identification: Selecting and articulating a problem to work on.

Separation: The development of metaphors separates the practitioner from his/her "conception" of the problem.

Development: Clean Language questions are asked to ascertain the attributes of any metaphors given. Metaphors are the embodied thoughts and feelings of the person. If one's metaphor features a rock, knowing what kind of rock it is makes a great difference. A sharp, jagged rock will perform a different service than a round smooth rock performs. This distinction becomes important during the next phase of the sequence.

Clean Language questions the facilitator poses to develop metaphors are:

And when you have ... where do you have ...?

And is it on the inside or the outside?

And does it have a size or shape?

And what's that like? And what kind of...
could that ... be?

And is there anything else about ...?

Maturation: The facilitator poses Clean Language questions to move time and eventually free the Figure Within. When time is moved, the Figure Within approaches "T," the worst moment of the experience. In the metaphoric story things get "worse" [emotionally more intense] until the practitioner crosses the threshold of "T." Once time begins to move forward, it is important to complete the session. Otherwise, the practitioner may experience his/her symptoms more intensely, as the Figure Within will be left at a time that is closer to the worst part of the experience.

Clean Language questions asked to move time are:

And what would ... like to have happen?

And what would ... like to do?

And what happens next?

And how long …?

And what happens after …?

Transformation/ Psychophysical Shift: Solutions arise. A psychophysical shift occurs in the session when the metaphors previously held in the body of the practitioner in T-1 transport into the ground [external environment] and transform. The practitioner feels this release physically, as if one's metaphorical "torch in throat" or "fist in stomach" were an object whose physical reality equaled any in the external world.

Proclamation: Within a session the individual "proclaims" nothing else needs to occur before the session ends. Proclamation continues as the practitioner works through the Reconstruction phase of the Resolution Sequence.

On the following pages you will find a Metaphor Map: a record of a Metaphor Session and the Case Study of an individual who combined Zen Meditation and Metaphor Awareness for twenty years. It offers evidence that individuals can work creatively and constructively with the karmic obstructions blocking their path to liberation. There are ways to encourage breakthrough. However, this comes with a word of caution. *Metaphors are powerful.* When we work metaphorically, *we will be changed.*

The only other work I have encountered that seems to be based on deep work with metaphors is *Feeding Your Demons: Ancient Wisdom for Resolving Inner Conflict* by Tsultrim Allione. The process is quite different from that of Metaphor Awareness but has the same potential for positive change. Tsultrim Allione also provides a method for the practitioner to work without a facilitator. This is something we have yet to develop for Metaphor Awareness.

Contained within the symptoms are
all the elements necessary to complete our healing.
—David Grove

Metaphor Awareness Map – Work on Trepidation

The metaphor map that follows is the verbatim record of a Metaphor Awareness session. The facilitator's questions will be prefaced with an F, the practitioner's response with P. Pauses within responses between words or phrases are indicated by ellipses […]. From time to time, comments by the facilitator about what is happening in the session will appear in italics.

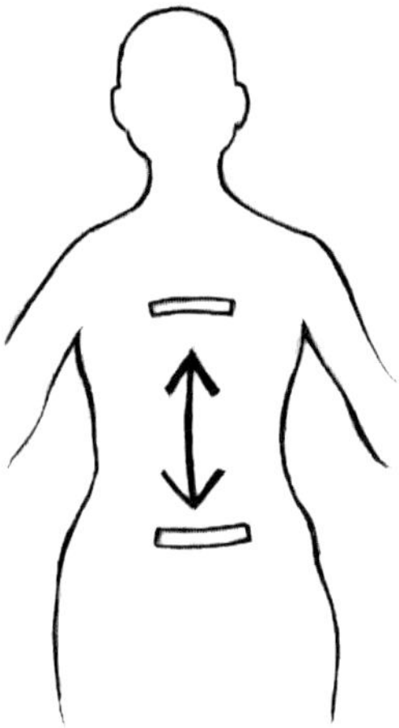

[F] And…what do you want…or what would you like to have happen?

[P] I would like to let go of the limiting effects of trepidation.

[F] And when you have trepidation… where do you have trepidation…when you have trepidation?

[P] In the middle of my body

[F] And when it's in the middle of your body…whereabouts is it…when it's in the middle of your body?

[P] From my breastbone to my navel

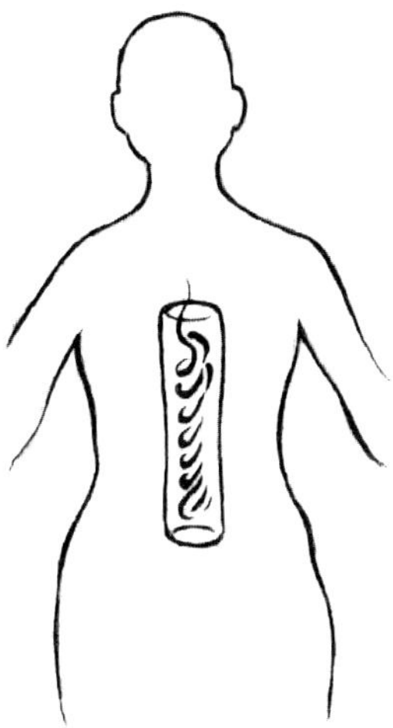

[F] And…when you have trepidation in the middle of your body between your breastbone to your navel…does it have a size or shape…or what's that like?

[P] It's like a hollow feeling on the inside…like a hollow tube…it's dark.

[F] And when it's like a hollow tube on the inside and it's dark…is there anything else about it?

[P] It has a quivery feeling to it…right in the middle…it makes me feel like crying.

[F] And…How old could you be… when you feel like crying?

The practitioner has indicated having a feeling about the hollow tube. The hollow tube is the adult's metaphor for trepidation. This feeling probably belongs to the Figure Within. The practitioner's voice changed with that statement, sounding small and timid compared to the previous responses. This is another indication of a Figure Within. The figure has emerged rather early in this session; it often takes more time to develop. In some sessions, no Figure Within appears, and Resolution occurs working with metaphors alone. Every session is completely unique, and what will develop is always a mystery.

[P] I'm three or four.

[F] And what could "three or four" be wearing?

"Three or four" is now the name of the Figure Within. Dressing the figure establishes rapport with that element and assists with the flow of information from it. There are three sources or containers of information: the individual to whom the event is happening [Figure Within], the individual's thoughts and feelings about what is happening [they will become metaphors], and the environment in which the event is occurring [ground]. Before the practitioner crosses "T," the information emerging is not linear and can be quite chaotic; it can quickly shift from one information source [figure, metaphor, or ground] to another. It can even change from one question to the next [as will be seen below].

[P] She is wearing a little summer outfit…with a bib front and suspenders…and no shirt. She has little white high-top shoes and white socks.

The specificity of detail that emerges in a session is often quite astounding. It is important to keep asking "And is there anything else" *until the practitioner says, "no."*

[F] And is there anything else about "three or four" when she's wearing … a little summer outfit with a bib front and suspenders and no shirt, and has white high-top shoes and white socks?

[P] She's sad…She feels like she's done something wrong but she doesn't know what it is.

"Three or four" is sad. The next thing that needs to be known is where "three or four" feels sad. Metaphors can now be developed for "three or four's" sadness. This information will be necessary for resolution.

[F] And when she feels sad…where is she sad…when she's sad?

[P] She's sad in the middle of herself and in her eyes.

The facilitator now goes to each location to develop metaphors.

[F] And when she's sad in the middle of herself…whereabouts in the middle…is she sad?

[P] In the middle…right here.

Practitioner points to the same area between the breastbone and navel.

[F] And when she's sad in the middle of herself… right here…does it have a size or shape? Or what's that like?

[P] It's like a little fledgling bird.

"Fledgling bird" is the first metaphor for "three or four's" sadness. The facilitator now moves on to the eyes because it was the second location

given for where she feels sad. Elements from both locations will be necessary in the session. In a Metaphor Awareness session, no information is superfluous. The facilitator worked to develop each metaphor in the order it first appeared: "middle of herself" followed by "in her eyes."

[F] And when she's sad in her eyes…what's that like?

[P] Like a waterfall of tears.

[F] And is there anything else?

[P] She's clinging to the side of the shaft…she doesn't know how she got there…she'd like to get out because it's dark.

All of a sudden we have a shift. And now we know where and why it is dark... "like a hollow tube...it's dark." Interestingly, "the hollow tube, it's dark" was the adult practitioner's metaphor for where she experienced trepidation. The hollow tube [shaft that is dark] is now the environment [ground] of the Figure Within. The information source has switched.

[F] And she's clinging to the side of the shaft, and she doesn't know how she got there … she'd like to get out … And is there anything else about a bird?

The facilitator now has a choice to make. She can investigate "dark," or work with the metaphors that have been given. She chooses the metaphors. This choice was made to more fully develop the bird before going into the dark. There are times when an inquiry garners no response from the practitioner. In that case, it is the facilitator's responsibility to find the next "right" question that can be answered. The information can circulate around.

Sometimes a question is just one or two inquires premature; it may not elicit a response the first time it was asked, but then, only one or two inquiries later, the practitioner responds quickly. This exemplifies the statement, "the practitioner learns to trust his/her own intuition and the autonomous nature of the healing process." There seems to be a precise pattern by which the information needs to reveal itself. Neither the facilitator nor the practitioner can know beforehand what that pattern is. The structure of the session and careful use of Clean Language assists the unfolding of information.

[P] It's a small bird…there is something wrong with one of its wings…it doesn't seem like it could be much help.

This refers back to the previous response, "she'd like to get out."

[P] It can cheep and cheep…it's been there a long time. Her throat is tight and keeps her from calling for help.

The figure within is only three or four years old. If the practitioner were thirty years old, say, or fifty, at the time of this session, the dynamic would have been in place for 26 or 46 years, respectively. So yes, it's been there for a long time!

[F] And when her throat is tight…what's that like?

[P] There's like a lump.

[F] And when…there's like a lump…what kind of lump could that lump be?

[P] It's like an egg…and if she swallows the tears and wets the throat she can swallow the egg.

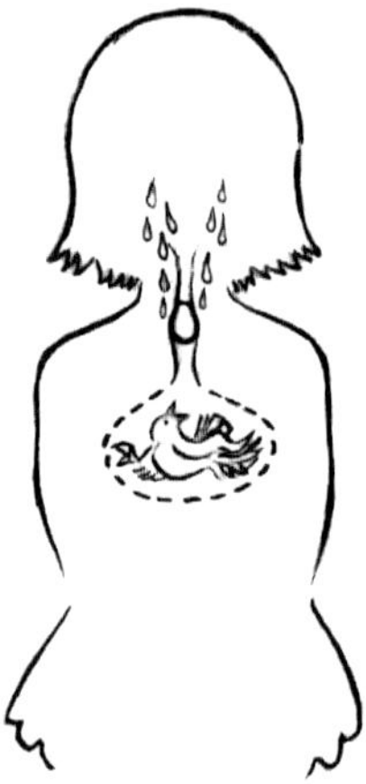

[F] And can that happen?

Solutions that are offered need to be checked to make sure they "can happen" within the session. Sometimes they cannot, the facilitator needs to explore combinations of other elements until the practitioner can respond. This is another indication of the precision of the information.

[P] Yes

[F] And what happens next when she can swallow the egg?

[P] The tears become salve for the bird's wing…and the bird can eat the nourishment of the egg and grow up.

The elements are combining and solutions are emerging. The tears now serve a beneficial purpose; they become salve for the bird's wing. The lump becomes an egg that can nourish the growing bird.

[F] And can that happen?

[P] Yes, the bird is getting better and stronger…the girl is in the well…there is not much around … she's afraid…it's the only thing she can do…she has to be there a long time and there is a lot of crying. She is still crying [T]. She is there so long.

This is the turning point in the session. The shaft has now become a well, a more defined element of the ground. Also, getting to the verb form "crying" is the penultimate moment before the worst moment. It is still the present experience of the Figure Within. She is still cry<u>ing</u>.

[F] And so what could happen so she wouldn't have to be there "so long?"

The facilitator works to move time forward, to assist in crossing the threshold of "T."

[P] A bird can grow up faster than a little girl.

[F] And a bird can grow up faster than a little girl… And what happens next when a bird can grow up faster than a little girl?

[P] The bird can fly away…it looks around for someone to help the little girl…Eventually there is a little calm because she knows the bird is trying to get some attention…but the well is in the middle of "nowhere."

The bird is looking for help and is no longer internal to "three or four." Instead it is in the environment where it belongs. A little girl

shouldn't have a bird in her "middle." Also, there is "a little calm." She is no longer crying because "the bird is trying to get some attention." Metaphorically, "three or four" has crossed T, the worst moment.

[F] And what happens next when a bird can fly away and looks around for someone to help the little girl?

[P] The bird goes to a father…but I don't know if he can help.

The practitioner has her eyes closed and describes a lot of "flickering" *and* "light and dark like a strobe light behind my eyes." *She takes this to be the quick passage of time,* "day/night and, day/night." *It goes on for a long time and* "it kinda hurts my eyes." *Intermittingly, she sees the faces of people she knows and others* "that must have been strangers I've seen at sometime in my life," *along with many images of animals. She states,* "I understand this to mean that it is taking many, many days, and the images are all the beings the bird tries to get to help." *All of a sudden, the bird comes back.*

[P] Now the bird is coming back with an elephant. She [*the elephant*] is very beautiful. The elephant belongs to the little girl, and the girl belongs to the elephant.

[F] And now the bird is coming back with an elephant … she is very beautiful. The elephant belongs to the little girl, and the girl belongs to the elephant … And what happens next?

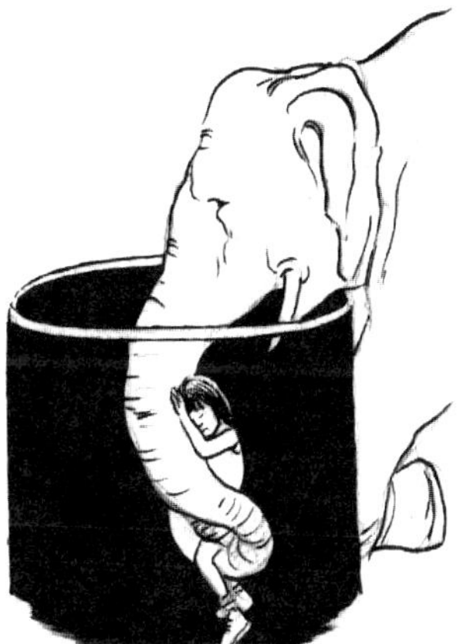

[P] The elephant kneels on her front legs and puts her trunk into the well and scoops the little girl up.

[F] The elephant kneels on her front legs and put her trunk into the well and scoops the little girl up … And then what happens?

[P] The elephant puts the little girl on her back and the little girl is happy. She gets to ride on the elephant. It's getting dark now and they need someplace to stay. She's not afraid. The bird is following them.

[F] *The facilitator repeats the practitioner's response* … And what else needs to happen?

[P] The well shaft is dangerous. It needs to be fixed so no one else can fall in there.

[F] *Practitioner's response is repeated* … And can that happen?

[P] Yes…workmen come and fill up the well with dirt and plant seeds so grass can grow over it.

[F] And is there anything else about a well that can be filled with dirt and seeds so grass can grow over it?

[P] All of a sudden the father is there and he likes flowers. He takes the little girl and they plant flowers together. The father doesn't see the elephant, but the little girl knows it's there.

The little bird is on the elephant's head… And the little girl is still afraid of that man.

[F] *Facilitator repeats the previous response* … And so…what could happen next when the little girl is still afraid of that man?

[P] The elephant is magical and changes into a beautiful woman. The father can see her. She's really kind and he is not angry at what she has to tell him…She tells him to manage his anger…the little girl doesn't understand it … and it makes her feel that she's bad. He gets it because she is not an ordinary person.

This solution has a magical/fairytale feel to it. That's because the Figure Within is only three or four years old. Solutions in a metaphor session are determined by what makes sense to the Figure Within. When the Figure Within is older, the solutions will be different and take forms appropriate to the developmental level of the internal figure.

[F] *Facilitator repeats previous response* ... And what happens next when he gets it?

[P] He picks up the little girl and twirls her in the sunshine, and she thinks she can trust that he has changed.

[F] And so...take some time to know how different it can feel...when a father can twirl a little girl in the sunshine, and she thinks she can trust that he has changed...And that's very different from clinging to the side of a dark well/shaft, isn't it?

This is called making words physical.

[P] Yes!

Here we have the beginning of the transformed landscape. There is sun, so it is no longer dark, and there is some changed ground outside of the place that used to be the well/shaft. There are flowers planted in the filled shaft.

[F] So take some time to know about that difference. Time is allowed. And so, what happens next?

[P] They walk away from that "no-place" and it begins to change. There is a neighborhood with a park and he takes her out for ice cream. They are holding hands.

The metaphoric landscape of "T+1" is filling in quite naturally. Information in a session flows more spontaneously in "T+1." In the "T-1" landscape, movement is dependent on the next "right" question.

[F] And they walk away from that "no-place" and it begins to change. There is a neighborhood with a park and he takes her out for ice cream, and they are holding hands …And does she like that?

[P] Oh yes! The ice cream is nice…healing the hollow space… filled with ice cream…and it doesn't really take that much.

The body is no longer host to a hollow space. The session is concluding. The facilitator checks on all the elements to see if anything else is needed. The more elements from the "T-1" landscape that can be transformed in the "T+1" landscape, the greater the healing. Some elements don't transform. They may be needed in future sessions. Elements that arise after "T" do not necessarily change. The elephant plays a role in subsequent sessions and does not transform. It appeared after the Figure Within passed through "T," although she was still in the same predicament. Things changed more easily after the elephant kneels down and "scoops the little girl up."

[F] And the ice cream is nice … healing the hollow space … filled with ice cream … and it doesn't really take that much … And what's happened to a little bird?

The little bird was an element in the "T-1" landscape. The facilitator checks to see if it changes form even though it changed by growing up and going into the environment.

[P] The little bird is changed. It is a big, beautiful crow now. It stays in a tree in the park. It can watch the little girl from there.

[F] And the little bird is changed. It is a big, beautiful crow now. It stays in a tree in the park. It can

watch the little girl from there. … And what's happened to the beautiful woman who is not an ordinary person?

[P] The elephant and the woman are both luminous and beautiful. They are made of light. They are the same thing in different forms…now it is just the elephant…it is very emotional and hard to explain. *The practitioner is tearful with a look of awe on her face.* I love them very much, and they love me.

[F] *Facilitator repeats previous response* … and what happens next?

[P] The little girl can grow up very fast. *I'm* standing facing the elephant. The love I feel for it is overwhelming. I have my hand on the side of its face, and its trunk curls around me. Nothing can be too bad when you have a friend like that.

The practitioner at first observes the little girl growing up very fast. All of a sudden it shifts to the adult practitioner, "I'm standing facing the elephant." So we've gone from "three or four" to the adult practitioner in an hour and a quarter. Before the session ends, the facilitator rechecks all elements one by one to see if anything else needs to happen.

[F] And does the little girl need anything else?

[P] No

[F] And does a father need anything else?

[P] No

[F] And do workmen need anything else?

[P] No

[F] And do flowers they planted need anything else?

[P] Yes, the flowers need rain so they can grow so no one would ever know a well-shaft was there.

[F] And the flowers need rain so they can grow … so no one would ever know a well/shaft was there … And can that happen?

[P] Yes

[F] And does a woman of light, that is not an ordinary person, need anything else?

[P] No

[F] And does a crow need anything else?

[P] No

[F] And does an elephant need anything else?

[P] No

[F] And does a hollow place between the breastbone and navel need anything else?

[P] No, it is filled.

[F] And do you need anything else?

This is addressed to the adult.

[P] No, I feel myself receding from the scene.

[F] And now that all this has happened, do you think you can let go of the limiting effects of trepidation?

[P] I think so. I guess I'll find out.

* * *

The practitioner reported significant change in the months following this Metaphor Awareness session. She said, "It's really subtle, though. If I weren't working with Reconstruction and the Resolution Sequence, I can see how you'd miss clarifying just what has changed. It all just feels so good and natural." She reported feeling less timid in social situations, and could risk disclosing more of herself. Her meditation felt more stable. Perhaps most importantly, she reported being less critical of herself, stating, "I'm not always worrying that I've done something wrong, like I used to."

Zen Meditation and Metaphor Awareness

A CASE STUDY 1991 – PRESENT

The following case study consists of a Zen practitioner's journal notes for some sixty Metaphor Awareness sessions in which he has participated since 1991. The information provided is by no means all-inclusive. It summarizes his reflections on the Metaphor Awareness process as a whole, the stages he has identified, and the nature of the changes he experienced during each phase. To this day, he continues to investigate the influence of Metaphor Awareness on his meditation practice and in his life.

At the time he began journaling about the process, the practitioner had been practicing Zazen for over twenty years. By then he had acquired mature observational skills, coupled with a comprehensive intellectual understanding of the basis of metaphor work. This provided him with a good foundation to develop a clear statement of what he wanted to work on through Metaphor Awareness. These skills greatly aided the ease and depth of the sessions, as well as the subsequent integration of new ways of being.

The practitioner engaged with his own, naturally arising koans. Once a problem had been clearly articulated, a Metaphor Awareness session was undertaken. The process of Metaphor Awareness easily transforms a conceptual problem into its metaphorical equivalent. Metaphors allow one to work directly with conditioning in ways that "thinking" about a problem does not accomplish. When the criteria for a complete session were met, the practitioner observed a desirable change. The time required to integrate these changes varied with each session.

The metaphor practitioner recounts the content of the sessions and their results in the first person. The facilitator's comments are in italics.

The Metaphor Awareness Work

Recognition of the Need for Action

My interest in working with the Metaphor Awareness process grew out of my need to find solutions to some life difficulties, as well as address physical symptoms that were unresponsive to medical treatment, meditative insight, or conventional psychological approaches. These included 1) an assortment of physical complaints [back, neck and abdomen, as well as various joint pains]; 2) a defensive attitude that inhibited my speaking freely; and 3) spontaneous visions of my father, who had been dead for forty years. The visions began when I reached the age he was at the time of his death.

My first sessions dealt with psychophysical discomfort. I had been receiving bodywork from a Trager practitioner and became aware of the relationship between my physical problems and some unresolved childhood experiences. It seemed as if the problems I experienced were the physical manifestations of the memories of emotional childhood pain. I questioned if it were possible to clear up some of the physical discomfort, would there be a psychological corollary? I found that there was.

Knowing there is a problem and identifying its physical and mental manifestations is the first step in the Metaphor Awareness process. For one first undertaking metaphor work, this can take time. Beginning practitioners should have a clear understanding of the dynamic they want to work on; work should begin with the Deconstruction side of the Resolution Sequence.

Personal Karmic Obstructions

Many early sessions were conducted to address my physical complaints. Most of the time, the metaphors took the form of cylinders, rods, metallic blades, rocks, and other rigid inanimate objects. At first they did not move easily because I lacked an understanding of the autonomous nature of the metaphors and their universal attribute of healing. I often consciously tried to define how a metaphor should move, rather than just observe without judgment the intuitional information that arose.

This interference disrupted an otherwise smooth transformational process. However, with time and experience, I learned to understand and deeply trust the intuitive wisdom of the metaphoric landscape. My trust grew from the positive results I experienced, and overrode my tendency to over analyze and create obstructions. It quickly became obvious that working with Metaphor Awareness brought relief from the negative effects [physical and mental] of conditioned states that I had coped with for many years.

Each session broadened my knowledge of the psychophysical nature of conditioned states, which manifest themselves both physically and psychologically. One can approach a problem either way. Once my work with Metaphor Awareness commenced, and I experienced relief from many aches and pains, my sense of well-being increased. Also during this period, the grief that underlay the visions of my deceased father were resolved. In fact, doing this work set me on the path to understanding the nature and source of many other problems.

One extremely important metaphor session occurred during this early stage. I was working with the desire to speak clearly, without self-consciousness or reticence. The metaphor for this problem expressed itself as a rag in my throat, choking off the free and natural functioning of my breath and voice. Elimination of the rag resulted in an ability to speak with greater clarity and freedom. Prior to its removal, my voice was always obstructed, my chanting atonal and discordant. Afterwards, it was as if an unnecessary appendage had been excised from my vocal cords. I could speak without undue hesitation and with fewer vocal pauses. Others [including my sister who didn't recognize me over the telephone] commented on how different my voice sounded. My atonal chanting improved, and I was able to develop my chanting skills far beyond what I had been capable of previously.

The practitioner's work brought a deeper understanding of how metaphors spontaneously move in concurrence with nonintrusive Clean Language inquiries. The skill of nonjudgmental attention, gained through the practice of Zazen, greatly aids metaphor work. Still, as stated above, it is only natural to need experience to gain trust in the metaphor process. For a practitioner to experience change, it is necessary to discern and accept what the metaphor "wants" to do over what one would prefer to have happen. After all, the individual has been coping with the problem since its inception, and, thus far, has not been able to resolve it.

Totem Figures

In time, my inanimate metaphors of metal and rock were replaced with animate beings, some mythological, as well as many common animals. I understood them to be expressions of the voice of nature, especially the common animals of my normal experience. Their appearance and generous assistance in a metaphor session helped redefine my attitude toward the world of nature. A fascination with nature replaced my fear of the natural world. My sense of separateness also diminished.

The way animals accept their lives and circumstances now stood out in stark contrast with my own tendency to resist my situation. The power of their being began to bring new functioning to my chakras. The previous work with inanimate metaphors cleared many blockages that had stopped the free flow of energy between them. I became aware of the subtle way that the chakras operated together—a sense of unity previously unobserved. One key metaphor that arose during this period expressed itself as a cave bear of immense size and strength. This cave bear rested in my heart chakra. Its presence enhanced inner authority and self-assurance. The *bear power* showed me how to deal with the hurtful projections of others by transforming negative emotions into understanding and compassion.

At this time, the practitioner began to report benefits to his meditation practice. He experienced a clearing of obstructions in the chakras, the place where a majority of the metaphors are initially located. He reported a slowing and deepening of his breath, allowing a new vigor while meditating. He found release from restlessness and tedium during Zazen.

Christian Symbols

I was raised Catholic and was always fond of some of the pre-Vatican II Latin ceremonies. I never experienced affinity for the crucifixion or resurrection, but the host in its various forms attracted my childhood religious imagination. For many metaphor sessions the host played a major transformational role, chief of which was its presentation in the Monstrance. The Monstrance is a golden vessel that is used in processions to carry and display a large consecrated host to the community. The host is held in the center of a golden circular spray behind a small glass door.

The Monstrance became a vehicle of inner transformation again and again, sometimes whole, sometimes as just the circular spray. The metaphor started to take on the shape of the host, one I take to be a symbol of wholeness. It moved between chakras providing further cleansing. Eventually the Monstrance, like the cave bear, came to rest in the heart chakra. At this time I began to sense the lower chakras as being filled with energy and completeness. My connection to the world at large was made through the solar plexus. I began to understand Right Action as "effortless" deeds that spring from a source of tranquility and insight deep within the *hara.*

About this time, I started to receive treatment from a cranial-sacral therapist. Visualization using color and forms was integral to the treatment, as well as some basic metaphor techniques. The visualizations came easily to me because of my prior work with Metaphor Awareness. During one of the treatments, the therapist requested of me to see what healing color was needed for a particular symptom. Instead of a color appearing, a vision of "helping hands" emerged. The hands assisted in taking out a foreign object from my neck and shoulder. These "helping hands" became a common occurrence, expressing themselves at the appropriate moment of healing. They responded with the same attributes of autonomous action as the metaphors. The "helping hands" first came and went by themselves, but later they became linked to my attention: that is, when I focused on a need they would appear and serve. Were they subject to my will? Not really. They responded to my call as it were, but acted within my field of attention without my guidance, performing healing far beyond what I could ever have imagined.

With the emergence of the "helping hands," a shift in the nature of the metaphor sessions occurred. Prior to their appearance each episode of metaphor work was self-contained or complete. Metaphors transformed and did not recur in future sessions. The recurrence of the hands in subsequent sessions was something new. The practitioner and facilitator discussed how to relate to the hands. Were they the practitioner's hands? No. Did he know whose hands they were? No. Until more could be learned, it was decided to relate to them with the same nonjudgmental attitude that is necessary for any metaphor work.

Other differences were noted. Prior to the "helping hands," the work dealt with the more gross forms of conditioned states, or with personal karma. Early sessions required a facilitator. Elements did not move unless the right questions were asked. Working with personal karma, resulted in positive changes to long -standing physical, emotional, and psychological difficulties. It was the remedial work necessary before "higher" transformational progress could be undertaken.

In studying the work since the appearance of the hands there is a qualitative difference in the results of metaphor sessions. After the appearance of the hands, sessions became even more transformational. Information moved more easily and needed less facilitator input. The results brought a more refined and subtle understanding of the nature of reality, one more in line with the universal perspective of the Buddhadharma. *Two examples are "Seeing" the nature of the universe as forgiveness, and "Witnessing" the voice of nature as a helping but never intrusive radiance.*

Buddhist Figures

At the onset of this stage, my metaphors formed and transformed in rapid-fire transitions. Previously, the facilitator's inquiries help precipitate their formation and movement. Now, however, the metaphors moved and transformed with a minimum of input, shifting form and place powered only by my inner attention. Many metaphors would form in my body [head and trunk] usually in association with one of the lower chakras [root, *hara*, or solar plexus]. They would then travel in the vital breath channel [the spine, head, and front of the body], sometimes exiting the body and returning to a different place from where they originated. In either case the changes would proceed rapidly.

After a while, the "helping hands" started to spontaneously take part in this process, moving the metaphors in and out of the body, as well as inside the body, from one chakra to another. The colors associated with these transformations changed from red and orange to yellow and blue. The "helping hands" were mostly "just hands." But, now, on occasion, the body associated with these hands would appear. It was a golden color and merged with my own body. This occurred a number of times.

As the process cleared the obstructions from my three lower chakras, the three higher chakras [throat, third eye, and aperture of Brahma] began to function in new ways. Golden Buddha figures began to come into view, and after a time one settled in my heart chakra. Zazen then consisted of the Golden Buddha supported by the cosmic *mudra* of my hands, with its body and head inwardly penetrating my body and head. The *Brahma Viharas* of kindness, compassion, sympathetic joy, and acceptance took on the additional universal attributes of healing and connectedness, forgiveness and harmony, gratitude and interdependence, and equanimity and intimacy.

The practitioner moved with ease within the metaphoric landscape and only related to the facilitator what was occurring.

Transformational Metaphors

In this stage, the speed and type of transformation changed again. The "helping hands" took on a larger, more creative role. In prior stages they moved metaphors from here to there, at times changing their forms by molding them into something else. Now the hands started to change their substance as well as their form. For example, a large, dark rocky ball appeared in the region of the solar plexus. The hands squeezed the ball into a small shape, pulled it out of the body through the solar plexus, and continued molding and rubbing it until it turned into a golden salve. The hands then rubbed the salve on my face and forehead. The salve was absorbed and became a vital breath that removed heretofore-unnoticed obstructions associated with the third eye and throat chakras. It then penetrated the remaining four lower chakras.

This process, and many others like it, moved quickly and with a minimum of input from the facilitator or me. The repetitive internal/external transformations seemed to break down the barrier that defines the boundary of the body. The body, as the container of consciousness, expanded beyond previously assumed limits. The boundaries of the physical body and consciousness could not be definitively determined. My "sense of self" was not limited to this "bag of skin" but embraced a large, unlimited space both within and outside my body. The seven chakras, now cleared of the gross obstructions by the actions of the metaphors and the "helping hands," related with new intimacy.

I noted a number of changes at this time. In particular, I experienced fewer hindrances to the processes of thought, breathing, and physical movements. Transformations proceeded even more rapidly. At the beginning of my involvement with Metaphor Awareness, a single session took 1 to 2 hours. Now one took fifteen to thirty minutes.

Almost always, transformations continue to involve the action of the "helpings hands." The hands seem to provide the exact creative action needed to change unwholesome materials into healing substances that are then placed into their "natural" spot.

Manifestations of Universal Wholeness

Two important sessions in the later stage resulted in the resolution of two major inquires that had been at the core of my practice for a long time.

1. One gave meaning to a comment made by a contemporary Zen Master during a private interview. He stated that, "The Buddhas are always with us." I questioned, "What does this mean, and how could one know that for oneself?"

2. The other gave rise to a new vision of *Buddhanature*, one that confirms the foundation of Buddhist morality has its root in the interplay of delusion and enlightenment.

These two key breakthroughs occurred within two months. Each breakthrough resolved longstanding questions. The results continue to be subtle changes in the perception of "reality" for the practitioner.

The Results of Integrating Zazen and Metaphor Awareness

Working with Metaphor Awareness greatly assisted the resolution of my personal karmic obstructions. Metaphor work had a profound effect on my Zazen practice and deepened my understanding of Buddhist truths. Each metaphor session heightened my sense of unity with the world. My confidence and trust in the complementary processes of Metaphor Awareness and Zazen increased, and my anxiety and doubt about Zazen practice diminished. Harmony of body and mind improved. The whole point of practice became clearer to me. Attaining dynamic stillness came with assuming the meditation posture, and then became possible at any time or circumstance by a simple act of attention.

Without the integration of Metaphor Awareness with my Zazen practice, I do not believe I would have been able to embody the changes that have occurred. Metaphor Awareness provided a method to permanently resolve identified barriers. Transformations in the metaphoric landscape most often remove the originating symptoms of the problem, and thus preclude its reoccurrence. Trusting the process allows one access to the wisdom of the nondual mind, and provides the means to creatively respond within the metaphoric landscape. The metaphors that arise through Clean Language questioning simultaneously embody the conditioned state and represent it symbolically; the symbol and the symbolized are thusness.[30] This being the case, Metaphor Awareness, and Dōgen's unity of practice/realization are understood as harmonious and mutually beneficial.

Endnotes

Introductory quote by Wolfgang Pauli

David Lindorf, *Pauli and Jung: The Meeting of Two Great Minds* [Wheaton, IL: Quest Books, 2004, p. 111]

Chapter 1 Introduction to *Tending the Fire*

1. Nishijima & Cross, *Master Dōgen's Shobogenzo: Book 1* [Charleston, S.C.: BookSurge, 1996, pp.15-16]

Chapter 2 Nonduality

2. Alex Bellos, *Here's Looking at Euclid* [New York: Simon & Schuster, Inc., 2010, pp. 123-125]
3. See Hsing Yun, trans. Tom Graham, *Buddhism: Core Ideas* [New York: Weatherhill, 2002, pp. 41-49] for a succinct yet thorough description of the Twelve Links and the methods to study them.
4. The explanation that the 2nd Link is the only place where the Chain can be broken is a practical device to facilitate an initial description. Actually, the Chain can be severed at any link providing an individual has the awareness, skill, understanding, and will to accomplish it. However, the perspective of this book is limited to the 2nd Link only.
5. Hee-Jin Kim, *Dōgen on meditation and thinking: a reflection on his view of Zen* [Albany, New York: State University of New York Press, 2007, p. 2]

Chapter 3 Nonduality—Resolution Sequence

6. It must be understood that not making preferences is an act of nonattachment that is concerned with internal events only. Zazen practice cultivates the nonpreferential attitude of mind. It does not mean to imply that having preferences in every day life is wrong. Successful living requires choices and decisions. Attempting to live without preferences as one performs life's duties leads to confusion and detrimental outcomes.

7. Zen Master Tung-shan, *The Song of the Jewel Mirror Awareness* [Ryumonji Zen Monastery Chant Book]

8. John Welwood, *Toward a Psychology of Awakening* [Boston & London: Shambhala, 2000, pp. 12-13]

9. Zen Master Tung-shan, *The Song of the Jewel Mirror Awareness* [Ryumonji Zen Monastery Chant Book]

10. Francesca Freemantle, *Luminous Emptiness* [Boston & London: Shambhala, 2001, p. 37]

11. See Robert Aitken, *Original Dwelling Place* [Washington, D.C.: Counterpoint, 1997, pp, 47-53] for his essay on the *Brahma Viharas*.

12. Francis Cook, *Hua-yen Buddhism* [University Park and London: Pennsylvania State University Press, 1977, p. 2] Indra's Net is an ancient Indian metaphor for reality taken up by the author(s) of the Avatamsaka Sutra and the Chinese philosophers of Hua-yen Buddhism as a means to visualize the intricate interdependence of life.

Indra's Net

> Far away in the heavenly abode of the great god Indra, there is a wonderful net that has been hung by some cunning artificer in such a manner that it stretches out infinitely in all directions. In accordance with the extravagant tastes of the deities, the artificer has hung a single glittering jewel in each eye of the net, and since the net itself is infinite in all dimensions, the jewels are infinite in number. There hang the jewels, glittering like stars of the first magnitude, a wonderful sight to behold. If we arbitrarily select one of the jewels for inspection and look closely at it, we will discover that in its polished surface there are reflected all the other jewels in the net, infinite in number. Not only that, but each of the jewels reflected in this one jewel is also reflecting all the other jewels, so that there is an infinite reflecting process occurring.

13. Ibid, p. 122.

14. Albert Low, *Hakuin on Kensho* [Boston & London: Shambhala, 2006, p. 103]

15. William R. LaFleur, *The Karma of Words: Buddhism and the Literary Arts in Medieval Japan* [Berkeley and Los Angeles: University of California Press, 1983, p. 93]

16. Kazuaki Tanahashi, *Enlightenment Unfolds: The Essential Teachings of Zen Master Dōgen* [Boston and London: Shambhala, 2000, p. 36]

Chapter 4 Natural Koan

17. Robert E. Buswell, *Tracing Back the Radiance* [Honolulu: University of Hawai'i Press, 1992, pp. 67-68]

    Buswell describes the differences between the "natural" koan of early Zen and their later development as "stylized" koan practice.

    > [Koan] practice was the product of a long process of development in the later Ch'an schools of the middle T'ang period in China. Most of the Ch'an schools during the T'ang were characterized by a close master/disciple relationship in which the master's influence and charisma played a central role in inspiring the student, instructing him in the practice, and finally catalyzing the ultimate realization, which is the goal of such practice. Many of the stories, which were transmitted about the direct instructions of the teachers, were recorded in a burgeoning literature exclusive to the Ch'an School. As the creative drive of the Ch'an waned after the mid-800s, later Ch'an masters began to draw upon the stories as teaching devices for their own students. [Teachers] used these stories as a systematic way of instructing their students, and began to collect them together in large anthologies. These stories began to be called *kung-an*, or "public case records," because they put an end to private understanding *(kung)* and are guaranteed to be in harmony with what the Buddhas and Ancestors would say *(an)*.

    Stylized Koan study is a beneficial tool of wisdom devised to aid students of Zen. It can be viewed as a substitute or addition to one's own naturally distilled life's question. Natural and Stylized together form a comprehensive overlay of skillful means that are available to modern day students of Zen.

18. Lafcadio Hearn, *In Ghostly Japan* [Rutland, Vermont & Tokyo, Japan: Tuttle Company, 1971, p.3]

19. Ibid, pp. 6-7.

20. For readers who are interested in understanding how we "smell our past lives" or skandhic memories as other Zen teachers refer to it, see Jiyu Kennet, *How to Grow A Lotus Blossom* [Mt. Shasta, California: Shasta Abbey, 1993, pp. 40-70]

21. Synonyms for Breakthrough include Transformation, Awakening, Nonduality, Liberation, Nirvana, Enlightenment, Thusness, Suchness, Emptiness, and Don't Know Mind.

Chapter 5 Employing the Resolution Sequence

22. Hara is the Japanese term used in Buddhism and the martial arts that refers to the part of the body about 3 inches below the navel. It is thought to be the reservoir of the subtle energy or life force called ch'i.

Chapter 6 *Shikantaza*

23. Hee-Jin Kim, *Dōgen on meditation and thinking: a reflection on his view of Zen* [Albany, New York: State University of New York Press, 2007, p. 100]

24. Ibid, p. 99.

25. William F Powell, *The Record of Tung-shan* [Honolulu: University of Hawai'i Press, 1986, p. 30]

26. Taigen Dan Leighton and Shohaku Okumura, *Dōgen's Extensive Record: A Translation of the Eihei Koroku* [Boston: Wisdom Publications, 2004, p. 91]

27. Zen Master Dōgen, *Fukanzazengi* [Ryumonji Zen Monastery Chant Book]

28. Ibid.

Appendix

29. In *Eihei Dōgen: Mystical Realist*, Dōgen scholar Hee-Jin Kim quotes Dōgen as saying, "We are not construing "like" as resemblance: "like" [nyo] is "thusness" [ze]." About this statement, Kim comments, " 'Like this' did not represent or point to thusness but *was* thusness.'" Hee-Jin Kim. *Eihei Dōgen: Mystical Realist* [Boston: Wisdom Publications 2004, p. 85]

30. "... And yet for him [Dōgen], symbol was to be realized as the expression of the symbolized. This was possible only when symbol was mediated,

liberated, and reinstated by the symbolized. Here we see Dōgen's creative and dynamic interpretation of the Buddhist doctrine of skillful means in which the means in question was not for the transcendence of duality so much as it was for the realization of it." Hee-Jin Kim. *Eihei Dōgen: Mystical Realist* [Boston: Wisdom Publications, 2004, p. 84]

BIBLIOGRAPHY

Aiken, Robert. *Original Dwelling Place.* Washington, D.C.: Counterpoint, 1997.

Allione, Tsultrim. *Feeding Your Demons: Ancient Wisdom For Resolving Inner Conflict.* New York: Little, Brown and Company, 2008.

Bellos, Alex. *Here's Looking at Euclid.* New York: Simon & Schuster, Inc., 2010.

Bielefeldt, Carl. *Dōgen's Manual of Zen Meditation.* Berkeley: University of California Press, 1988.

Cook, Francis H. *Hua-yen Buddhism: The Jewel Net of Indra.* University Park and London: Pennsylvania State University Press, 1977.

____________________. *Sounds of Valley Streams: Translation of Nine Essays from Shobogenzo.* Albany, New York: State University of New York Press, 1989.

Dumoulin, Heinrich. *Zen Buddhism: A History Volume 2 Japan.* New York: Macmillan Publishing Company, 1990.

Fremantle, Francesca. *Luminous Emptiness.* Boston & London: Shambhala Publications, 2001.

Grove, David. *Training Module 1: In the Presence of the Past.* David Grove Seminars.

_______________. *Training Module 2: Reweaving A Companionable Past.* David Grove Seminars.

_______________. *Training Module 3: And Death Shall Have No Dominion.* David Grove Seminars.

Hearn, Lafcadio. *In Ghostly Japan.* Rutland, Vermont & Tokyo, Japan: Charles E. Tuttle Company, 1971.

Katagiri, Dainin. *Each Moment Is The Universe.* Boston & London: Shambhala Publications, 2007.

Kennet, Jiyu. *How to Grow a Lotus Blossom or How a Zen Buddhist Prepares for Death.* Mt. Shasta, California: Shasta Abbey, 1993.

Kim, Hee-Jin. *Dōgen on meditation and thinking: a reflection on his view of Zen.* Albany, New York: State University of New York Press, 2007.

_______________. *Eihei Dōgen: Mystical Realist.* Boston: Wisdom Publications, 2004.

Lawley, James and Penny Tompkins. *Metaphors in Mind: Transformation Through Symbolic Modeling.* London: The Developing Company Press, 2000.

Leighton, Taigen Dan and Shohaku Okumura. *Dōgen's Extensive Record: A Translation of the Eihei Koroku.* Boston: Wisdom Publications, 2004.

Lindorff, David. *Pauli and Jung: The Meeting of Two Great Minds*. Wheaton, IL: Quest Books, 2004.

Loori, John Daido. *Sitting with Koans*. Boston: Wisdom Publications, 2006.

___________________. *The Art of Just Sitting: Essential Writings on the Zen Practice of Shikantaza*. Boston: Wisdom Publications, 2002.

___________________. *The True Dharma Eye: Zen Master Dōgen's Three Hundred Koans*. Boston & London: Shambhala Publications, 2005.

Low, Albert. *Hakuin on Kensho: The Four Ways of Knowing*. Boston & London: Shambhala, 2006.

Loy, David. *Nonduality: A Study In Comparative Philosophy*. Amherst, New York: Humanity Books an imprint of Prometheus Books, 1988.

Nishijima, Gudo & Chodo Cross. *Master Dōgen's Shobogenzo: Book 1*. Charleston, South Carolina: BookSurge, LLC, 1996.

______________________________. *Master Dōgen's Shobogenzo: Book 2*. Charleston, South Carolina: BookSurge, LLC, 1996.

______________________________. *Master Dōgen's Shobogenzo: Book 3*. Charleston, South Carolina: BookSurge, LLC, 1997.

______________________________. *Master Dōgen's Shobogenzo: Book 4*. Charleston, South Carolina: BookSurge, LLC, 1999.

Powell, William F. *The Record of Tung-shan.* Honolulu: University of Hawaii Press, 1986.

Sullivan, Wendy and Judy Rees. *Clean Language: Revealing Metaphors and Opening Minds.* Wales, UK & Bethel, CT: Crown House Publishing Limited, 2008.

Tanahashi, Kazuaki. *Enlightenment Unfolds: The Essential Teachings of Zen Master Dōgen.* Boston & London: Shambhala Publications, 2000.

Yun, Hsing. Trans. Tom Graham. *Buddhism: Core Ideas.* New York: Weatherhill, 2002.

___________________________________. *Describing the Indescribable.* Boston: Wisdom Publications, 2001.

___________________________________. *Lotus In A Stream.* New York: Weatherhill, 2000.

Welwood, John. *Toward a Psychology of Awakening.* Boston & London: Shambhala Publications, 2000.

About the Authors

Dale Verkuilen has been a Zen practitioner since 1968, Barbara since 1971. They met and married in 1974. Both are ordained Soto Zen priests. They have studied with a number of pioneering Japanese priests, as well as accomplished American teachers. The Verkuilens co-founded the Midwest Soto Zen Community in 2001. *Tending the Fire: An Introspective Guide to Zen Awakening* is their first co-authored book. Barbara is the author of *The Tale of Zen Master Bho Li*, and *Dokusan with Dogen: Timeless Lessons in Negotiating the Way*. Dale is currently working on his second book, *Unfolding the Eightfold Path: A Contemporary Zen Perspective.*

The Verkuilens live in Madison, Wisconsin. Their books are available at Firethroat Press, www.FirethroatPress.com.